A SONG
in the
FURNACE

The Message of the Book of Daniel

LAWRENCE R. FARLEY

ANCIENT FAITH PUBLISHING
CHESTERTON, INDIANA

A Song in the Furnace: The Message of the Book of Daniel
Copyright ©2018 by Lawrence R. Farley

Published by:
    Ancient Faith Publishing
    A Division of Ancient Faith Ministries
    P.O. Box 748
    Chesterton, IN 46304

ISBN: 978-1-944967-31-4

Printed in the United States of America

Contents

*Dedicated to
the people of the furnace,
the Christian martyrs of the twenty-first century*

INTRODUCTION

The Message of the Book of Daniel

THE LONGER I LIVE AND THE MORE THE DAYS DARKEN in the world around us, the louder and more urgent the message of the Book of Daniel becomes, and the more I come to identify with its central protagonists. Like Daniel, we also live in Babylon, awaiting its apocalyptic fall, and like Daniel's three holy and youthful friends, we also increasingly stand face to face with Nebuchadnezzar as he demands our cultural submission to an alien ideology.

It was ever thus for the Church: in the days before Constantine bestowed the gift of peace, Christians faced the demand from the powers ruling Babylon the Great that we worship the beast, burning incense to acknowledge his sovereignty (Rev. 17:5). In a later day, Christians were faced with the imperial demand to bow before the official policy of iconoclasm. Later still the Christians in communist Russia faced the State's demand to embrace the reigning atheist socialist ideology. Nebuchadnezzar, it seems, is not simply an historical figure. He is an eternal *zeitgeist*, the spirit of the age, and he confronts the three young men of God in every historical epoch. Even now we Christians in the West stand before him and his monstrous image and hear him bellow his timeless demand for submission to the currently reigning ideology of perverted secularism.

This then is the urgent message of the Book of Daniel. As we stand before the powers of the age and hear the demand for cultural assimilation and surrender to secularism, we must make our own the words of the three young men to the king as the furnace of fury burned before them: "We have no need to answer you in this matter. If it be so, our God whom we serve is able to deliver us from the burning fiery furnace, and He will deliver us out of your hand, O king. But if not, be it known to you, O king, that we will not serve your gods or worship the golden image that you have set up" (Dan. 3:16–18).

There will, of course, for us as for them, be a price to be paid for such cultural defiance. It may be death (as in the pagan days of the early Church) or exile (as in communist Russia). It may involve fines or social stigma, loss of job or income. It may simply involve being unpopular and marginalized, living as a kind of social pariah. Nebuchadnezzar's furnace has burned throughout the centuries with various kinds of flames. But a cost of some kind will certainly be exacted if we Christians remain true to our Orthodoxy and our timeless and unchanging Apostolic Tradition.

And what will we do when cast into the midst of those flames? We will not cower or cringe, retreating into a kind of cultish paranoia, looking back at the persecuting world with bitter and angry denunciation. We will do what the three holy youths did in the furnace, and what the Church has always done when it finds itself cast into the fire: we will sing. "Blessed are You, O Lord God of our fathers, for You are praiseworthy and exalted beyond measure unto the ages!" (Dan. 3:52). We will still give to the world a reason for the hope that is in us (1 Pet. 3:15), but our heart and focus will not be on this world, but on the world to come. We will survive the fiery furnace, for like the friends of Daniel, we have with us in that blaze one whose appearance is like the Son of God (compare Dan. 3:25).

The Book of Daniel: Israel in Wonderland

From the early days in the Church's history, from at least the time of the Church's critic Porphyry (c. AD 234–305), the Book of Daniel has come under attack. Porphyry, for example, derided the Christians for their use of the Book of Daniel and declared that the book did not contain genuine predictive prophecy but was in fact written after the historical events predicted and so was a fraud.

This pagan critic of old has had many followers, liberal scholars who also delighted to find "mistakes" in the history of the sacred text and who thus implicitly denied that the Book of Daniel was the Word of God. The results of such criticism were predictable: Christians in Porphyry's day and later rushed to the barricades to defend its historicity and attempt to explain away the apparent mistakes in the historical narrative which the liberals had found.

The Book of Daniel thus quickly became not so much a series of stories to be read with delight as a series of mistakes to be explained away; it became an arena in which liberals and conservatives traded scholarly bare-knuckle blows in their attempts to either discredit the book as merely another piece of ancient literature or else vindicate it as the true and authentic Word of God. Such was the noise and ferocity of the fight that one apologist for the book's historical authenticity, Josh McDowell, entitled his work *Daniel in the Critics' Den*. And it has to be admitted that the liberal lions were roaring pretty loudly.

The problem with such noisy warfare is that it puts the devout reader in serious danger of missing the magic and of misreading the text. To fully and truly appreciate the Book of Daniel, I suggest wresting the book for a while from both its liberal critics and its conservative defenders and putting it into the hands of a child. That is, I suggest that an invaluable perspective on the Book of Daniel could be gained by reading the stories to a child and making notes on the child's reaction. For the child, mercifully immune to the strife of scholars and cheerfully deaf to the noise of polemics, can appreciate the Book of Daniel for what it really is: a book of exciting adventures, a series of stories filled with miracles and thrills, a collection of visions and visits by angels.

The stories of the Book of Daniel are all larger than life—the villains, the plots, the heroes, the miraculous rescues, the angels and the visions they bestow—everything is of unheard-of and gigantic proportions. Opening the Book of Daniel, one falls down a literary rabbit hole into an exilic wonderland, a world full of monstrous statues and fiery furnaces and roaring lions and angels and visions. Kings threaten courtiers with death and have dreams; they almost turn into animals and are restored. The Book of Daniel is stuffed to overflowing with such *mirabilia*, and it is these which entrance the child and are meant to inspire us. This is the first and most fundamental fact about the book, and if we miss this, we misunderstand what the book is all about. Certainly we adults must bring the weight of history and the insights of scholarship to bear on the book in our reading. But we must never let these cause us to mislay the wonder the book is meant to arouse in us, for if we do, our scholarship will lead us astray.

Let us take one example among many possible ones. In the third chapter of the Book of Daniel, we read of the erection of a golden image whose height was sixty cubits—that is, about ninety feet. This was of eerily monstrous size in the ancient world, since even the Colossus of Rhodes, one of the Seven Wonders of that world, was about 108 feet high. The fact that its width was only six cubits (nine feet) merely added to the unnatural eeriness of the whole thing. How could such a thing exist? Here is where the strife of scholars begins to lead us astray, not only from the wonder of the child but even from the literal text. Liberal scholars deride the story for the impossible dimensions of the image, and conservatives rush to defend those dimensions. How could an image possibly be that tall? Perhaps, opine some conservative scholars, the sixty cubits of its height included a tall base or pedestal. The image itself might not have been sixty cubits tall—the pedestal, however, was very tall, and this height was included by the sacred narrator when he recorded its historical dimensions.

The explanation, however, flies in the face of what the text actually says when it records that "Nebuchadnezzar made an image of gold, whose height was sixty cubits" (Dan. 3:1). By trying to make the story conform to the more sober possibilities of history and thus salvage its historicity, the explanation also removes the element of wonder from the story and sets us up to misread it. The story of the three young men in the fiery furnace concerns the creation of an unnatural and monstrous golden statue, a thing so tall as to be terrible. The difficulty of constructing something at once so tall and so comparatively narrow is meant to compound and intensify the terror. We miss all this and cannot taste the story properly if we begin to alter its details to make them conform to what we regard as more historically likely.

The sacred author presents us with an amazing image of almost supernatural proportions and sets us up to wonder—not just at the size of the image, but also at the heroism of the protagonists. To read the story as the author intended and to appreciate it for the literature it is, we must enter into the world of the story as given. The author tells us the terrible image was sixty cubits tall. We are meant to look way up and tremble and reflect on the invincible might of a king who could build such a monstrous image—not whittle the thing down to size by talking about a possible pedestal.

It is the contention of this volume that both liberals and conservatives, by focusing so determinedly upon issues of historicity, miss the magic and misread most of the message. Issues of date, author, and genre will be examined with other reflections at the conclusion.[1] For such issues are best left to the end, after evidence from the text has been examined; otherwise, one might more easily succumb to the temptation of reading the text in light of one's presuppositions and not basing one's conclusions upon a reading of the text. Since the Book of Daniel is part of God's Word and is Holy Scripture, we must let it speak to us with its own voice and not attempt to tame it so as to try to make it fit into the historical boxes we have made for it. God's Word is not so easily tamed. We must put aside our presuppositions to listen attentively to all that Scripture says.

A Few Technical Matters

The commentary will be based on the Hebrew/Aramaic text rather than on the Old Greek version or the later Theodotian Greek text that replaced it (sometimes referred to erroneously as the Septuagint). These latter two Greek versions differ dramatically from one another and also from the Hebrew/Aramaic text. They both contain the so-called "Additions to the Book of Daniel" (the "Prayer of Azariah" and the "Hymn of the Three Young Men" in chapter three, and "Susannah" and the story of "Bel and the Serpent" usually appended at the end). These will also be examined in the commentary. These Greek additions are clearly later than the original Semitic text of Daniel and breathe a different spirit. For this reason the commentary is based on the Hebrew/Aramaic text as the more original.

The translation of the Hebrew/Aramaic offered here is my own. The translation of the Greek additions is my revision of the Revised Standard Version. (The list of the commentaries and works consulted can be found at the end.)

---

1   Matters of historical difficulty will be noted in passing in footnotes like this one.

The text of Daniel will be inset in blocks to clearly differentiate text from commentary. Parts of the Book of Daniel cited in the commentary will be indicated **by a bold font, like this.**

Also, as mentioned above, parts of the Book of Daniel were written in Hebrew and other parts in Aramaic. Such changes are usually signaled in our Bibles by a marginal note indicating where the change in language begins. In this commentary the change from one language to another will be indicated by a change of font, with the Hebrew text written in the same font as the main text, while the Aramaic portions of the text are given in the Legacy Sans font like this. The Additions to the Book of Daniel, translated from the Greek, are in the Function font like this.

WE HAVE SAID THAT THE BOOK OF DANIEL IS A THRILLING book of adventures, a book of harrowing dangers and supernatural escapes, a series of stories to widen the eyes and take one's breath away, a time spent in wonderland. Let us open the book now and plunge down the rabbit hole with Daniel and his friends. A whole new world awaits us—a world that reveals that God never abandons His people, no matter in which world they dwell.

PART 1

Daniel and His Friends Come to the King's Court in Babylon

Entering the King's Service

God Rewards Daniel for Resisting the King's Foreign Food

1 ¹In the third year of the reign of Jehoiakim, king of Judah, Nebuchadnezzar king of Babylon came to Jerusalem and besieged it. ²And the Lord gave Jehoiakim king of Judah into his hand, with some of the vessels of the house of God, which he carried to the land of Shinar to the house of his god; and he brought the vessels into the treasury of his god. ³Then the king commanded the major-domo, the chief of his eunuchs, to bring some of the sons of Israel and some of the king's descendants and some of the nobles, ⁴youths in whom there was no blemish, but handsome, understanding in all wisdom, having knowledge and quick to learn, competent to serve in the king's palace, and whom they might teach the literature and language of the Chaldeans. ⁵And the king assigned them a daily portion of the king's rich food which he ate and of the wine which he drank, and to train them for three years, so that at the end of that time they might stand before the king. ⁶Now from among those of the sons of Judah were Daniel, Hananiah, Mishael, and Azariah. ⁷For them the chief of the eunuchs decided on names: for Daniel he decided on the name Belteshazzar; for Hananiah, Shadrach; for Mishael, Meshach; and for Azariah, Abed-Nego.

The Book of Daniel opens with a poignant and painful memory—a backward glance to a time of separation, exile, and heartbreak. The narrator takes his reader back to the land of Israel, back to their home in a happier day, a time before defeat, death, national extinction, and exile. The reader stands **in the third year of the reign of Jehoiakim, king of Judah**—that is, in about the year 606 BC. The tribe of Judah then still lived in their ancestral land, and the temple was still functioning, the smoke of its sacrifices still rising from its altar and offering access to God's saving Presence. Yet all would soon change, for in that third year of Jehoiakim's reign, **Nebuchadnezzar king of Babylon came to Jerusalem and besieged it**.

Here, right at the outset of the narrative, we come upon our first historical difficulty, for Nebuchadnezzar actually did not besiege Jerusalem in the third year of Jehoiakim's reign, in 606 BC, but later, in the reign of Jehoiachin, in 598–597.[2]

The whole narrative is meant to conjure up feelings of shame and humiliation. A hateful and strutting pagan came to the holy land, and God **gave** not only Israel's anointed king **into his hand**, but

---

2   In 2 Kings 24 we read only that Jehoiakim rebelled against the rule of
     Nebuchadnezzar, not that Nebuchadnezzar besieged Jerusalem and conquered
     it. The text in 2 Kings 24 relates that it was only during the next reign, that
     of Jehoiachin in 598–597 BC, that Nebuchadnezzar's forces besieged and
     took Jerusalem (v. 10). It is quite unlikely that such a previous siege and
     catastrophe as Daniel here mentions would be unrecorded in the account
     of 2 Kings. In fact, contemporary Babylonian records of the time mention
     no siege of Jerusalem until that of 598 BC, during the reign of Jehoiachin.
     This is confirmed by Jer. 36:9f, which shows that even by the fifth year
     of Jehoiakim's reign Judah had not yet been invaded. It could be that the
     reference in Daniel 1:1 to deportation in Jehoiakim's third year was inspired
     by a comparison of a mention of Jehoiakim's deportation (in 2 Chr. 36:6)
     with a mention of his serving Nebuchadnezzar "for three years" (in 2 Kin.
     24:1)—i.e., Jehoiakim served Nebuchadnezzar for three years, after which he
     rebelled and was deported.

also **some of the vessels of the house of God, and he brought the vessels into the treasury of his god**. The mention of Nebuchadnezzar's **god** is repeated twice (referring to both **the house of his god** and **the treasury of his god**), to stress the sacrilege of it all. It is as if one can still feel the burning shame of exile—the holy vessels, commanded to be handled only by God's priests, were **carried to the land of Shinar** (note the anachronistic name of Babylon, as cited from Genesis 11:2, the place of ancient rebellion against God), the land of idols and provocative pride.

And not the vessels only, but the human treasures of the holy people were also taken as plunder: **the king commanded the majordomo,[3] the chief of his eunuchs, to bring some of the sons of Israel to serve in the king's palace**. With these few words the narrator skillfully builds up a picture of shame for the disgraced exiles. The transfer of population was not an unusual practice. The best and the brightest among the conquered people were given an opportunity to serve and advance in their new land among their captors. Here this involved them learning **the literature and language of the Chaldeans**—that is, becoming familiar and fluent in the Akkadian language and with a pagan culture of the priestly caste. This reeducation and assimilation into Babylonian society meant that the young men were given a **daily portion of the king's rich food which he ate and of the wine which he drank** as their usual food while he undertook to **train them for three years**. The new food and drink mirrored their new situation. And though not intended by the Babylonian masters, the temptation of the exiles to apostatize and forget their former holy heritage was built in.

Among this multitude of exiles from the kingdom of **Judah** were **Daniel, Hananiah, Mishael, and Azariah**, all probably about

---

3   Heb. *ashpenaz*, an Old Persian term meaning "innkeeper," taken as a proper name in the translations.

fourteen years old, the usual age for young boys being trained for such work. All that was familiar and safe for them had now been replaced by what was foreign, even down to their new names. For the narrator says that the **chief of the eunuchs decided** to give them all new **names: for Daniel the name Belteshazzar**; for **Hananiah,** the name **Shadrach**; for **Mishael,** the name **Meshach**, and for **Azariah,** the name **Abed-Nego**. No insult or degradation was of course meant by such renaming; it was natural that courtiers in Babylon should be called by good Babylonian names, not by (to them) foreign-sounding Jewish ones. One could even consider the naming a mark of advancement and acceptance on the part of their new hosting culture.

But even so, the names aggravated their sense of exile, and all the more so since they involved the names of pagan deities. Daniel's old name meant "God is my judge"; his new name, however, incorporated the name of the Babylonian deity Bel (or Marduk). The name Shadrach possibly meant "command of Aku" (the Babylonian moon god). The name Azariah meant "Yahweh has helped"; his new name "Abed-Nego" meant "servant of Nabu," another god in the Babylonian pantheon. (It is possible that the narrator deliberately misspelled the Babylonian names, in an act of disrespect for those foreign deities.)

Thus everything had changed for these young men—they had lost their home, their access to the temple, their vernacular, their diet, even their names. The temptation to apostatize and to forget Jerusalem (Ps. 137:5) was strong. The stage was set. What would they do?

[8] But Daniel decided in his heart that he would not defile himself with the portion of the king's rich food, nor with the wine which he drank. Therefore he requested of the chief of the eunuchs that he might not defile himself. [9] Now God had brought Daniel into the favor and compassion of the chief of the eunuchs. [10] And the

chief of the eunuchs said to Daniel, "I fear my lord the king, who has appointed your food and your drink. For why should he see your faces looking worse than the youths who are your own age? So you would endanger my head to the king." ¹¹ So Daniel said to the steward whom the chief of the eunuchs had appointed over Daniel, Hananiah, Mishael, and Azariah, ¹² "Please test your servants for ten days, and let us be given vegetables to eat and water to drink. ¹³ Then let our appearance be examined before you, and the appearance of the youths who eat the portion of the king's rich food; and according to what you see, so deal with your servants." ¹⁴ So he listened to them in this matter and tested them for ten days.

It is here, at this first challenge, that we see the courage of the exiles. If the chief of the eunuchs decided on names (v. 7), Daniel also **decided** something—namely **that he would not defile himself with the portion of the king's rich food, nor with the wine which he drank**. Why, we may ask, did Daniel and his friends find this food objectionable? The term "defile" is a strong one; in Isaiah 59:3 it is used to describe the sin of murder. Though certainty eludes us, it seems that Daniel found the food unacceptable because of the possibility that it had been offered to idols, since meat and wine were staples of such sacrifices in a way that vegetables were not.

The idea of the uncleanness of Gentile food was part of Jewish postexilic culture. This is reflected in the Book of Tobit, where Tobit says, "When I was taken captive to Nineveh, all my brothers ate from the bread of the Gentiles, but I protected myself by not eating it, for I remembered God" (Tobit 1:10–12). In the Book of Judith, Judith brings her own Jewish food with her into the Gentile camp, lest eating the Gentile food be an "offense" (Judith 12:1f).

One can see the deepest purpose of the narrator, however, by comparing Daniel's scruples with those of the Jews persecuted by

Antiochus Epiphanes in the second century BC. That notorious Gentile tyrant then tempted Jews to apostatize by forcing them to eat unclean food. Thus we read that "Eleazar, one of the scribes in high position, was forced to open his mouth to eat swine's flesh. But welcoming an honorable death rather than a defiled life, he spat out the meat" (2 Macc. 6:18–19). And not Eleazar only, but "many in Israel grew strong and determined in themselves not to eat unclean things. They chose to die rather than be defiled by foods or profane the holy covenant" (1 Macc. 1:62–63). Those reading this story in the times of the Maccabees would have found courage in Daniel's refusal to eat unclean food.

Rather than outright refusing the food (and endangering himself and his companions by his defiance), Daniel humbly **requested of the chief of the eunuchs** responsible for his food that he be allowed an alternative diet. Not unnaturally, Daniel's superior was reluctant to accede to the request, lest the king **should see your faces looking worse** than others in training, and he bear the brunt of the king's displeasure for the decision. In fact, if the king found his charges looking worse than others, he would cut off the chief's head (v. 10). This seems rather an extreme penalty for such a minor offense, but royal extremism and tyrannical terrorism are literary commonplaces in such stories as this. The threat of death in the event of failure serves to heighten the drama and contribute to the overall tension and excitement of the tale.

Once again Daniel does not insist on getting his way nor take a self-righteous stand on his principles. Rather, he trusts in God to change the mind of those responsible for him. **"Please,"** he says, **"test your servants for ten days."** (Note the gracious humility of the request.) Then, he says, if after even such a short period on the alternate diet they are worse off, they will comply and eat the original fare as provided. The contest is set, and the clock begins to tick.

Will Daniel and his friends indeed be worse off for their vegetarian diet? Will they be forced to defile themselves after all? Will the great and important chief of the eunuchs have to die?

We miss the feel of the tale if we minimize this episode and regard it as a minor issue regarding personal scruple. The narrator presents this first story as a matter of life and death in a foreign land. As such, it foreshadows all the other stories in the Book of Daniel regarding life and death, such as the stories of the fiery furnace and the lions' den. This test about food is in reality a test about whether to sacrifice piety and principle in order to gain worldly advancement. It is the opening shot in a counter-challenge of faith against apostasy—a counter-challenge that would find final fruition in the Maccabean resistance. We should not minimize the story's importance simply because the threat of death would fall upon the chief of the eunuchs rather than upon Daniel and his friends.

> [15] And at the end of ten days their appearance looked better and fatter in flesh than all the youths who ate the portion of the king's rich food. [16] Thus the steward took away their portion of delicacies and the wine that they were to drink, and gave them vegetables. [17] As for these four youths, God gave them knowledge and skill in all literature and wisdom; and Daniel had understanding in all visions and dreams. [18] Now at the end of the days, when the king had said to bring them in, the chief of the eunuchs brought them in before Nebuchadnezzar. [19] Then the king spoke with them, and among them all none was found like Daniel, Hananiah, Mishael, and Azariah; therefore they stood before the king. [20] And in all matters of wisdom and understanding about which the king examined them, he found them ten times better than all the astrologers and enchanters who were in all his kingdom. [21] Thus Daniel continued until the first year of King Cyrus.

The narrator breaks the built-up tension and reports that at the end of ten days, Daniel and his friends **looked better and fatter in flesh than all the youths who ate the portion of the king's rich food.** They passed the test! (And, though this is not emphasized by the narrator, the chief of the eunuchs got to retain his head.) It seems there is at least an element of God's supernatural provision in the result of their simple diet, since a mere ten days would not necessarily result in someone becoming better in appearance and fatter in flesh than others. Just as God would supernaturally bestow insight into dreams, immunity from a fiery furnace, and safety among lions, so He begins to work supernaturally here by bestowing upon these young men visibly better health than everyone else, and this after a mere week or so.

Ultimately, of course, the story is not about the heroism of Daniel and his friends or about the superiority of the Jewish diet. Rather, it is about the gracious rescue of God. God had brought Daniel into the favor (Heb. *hesed*) and compassion of the chief of the eunuchs. Then He bestowed radiant appearances upon Daniel and his friends when they trusted in Him to do so. The action of the steward after that, in taking away the prescribed royal diet and permanently giving them vegetables, should not be regarded merely as everyone recognizing the outcome of a superior diet, but as the work of God and His reward for His servants when they refused to conform to the pagan idolatry around them.

The story concludes with other rewards from God. Not only did He save them from defiling themselves with food because they stood firm against idolatry, but also **God gave them knowledge and skill in all literature and wisdom.** Furthermore, **Daniel had understanding in all visions and dreams**. This knowledge was not the result of diligent study in Chaldean lore (though of course such study would have been required of Daniel and his companions). It

also was the gift of God, from whom come all wisdom and knowledge. Not surprisingly, when **at the end of the days** (i.e., at the conclusion of their three years' training; v. 5) they were interviewed to
determine their fitness for serving at court, **among them all none
was found like Daniel, Hananiah, Mishael, and Azariah**. It was
the king himself who examined them, and **he found them ten
times better than all the astrologers and enchanters who were
in all his kingdom**. Such excellence could only have come as a special gift from God.

We note here too an element of hyperbole. Not only are such
minor and unimportant figures as exiled youths interviewed by
the king himself, these four stand out visibly from all the other
exiles and trainees. And not only that, when they at length were
brought to court to serve (lit., to stand **before the king**), the king
found these older teens **ten times better than all the astrologers
and enchanters who were in all his kingdom**. The young men,
lacking age and experience, radically outstripped all the professionals with years of it. The account here reads like a romance.

It ends by saying that Daniel **continued until the first year of
King Cyrus**, serving at the Babylonian court from 606 until 538
BC, by which time he was an old man. That is, he outlasted the
Babylonian court and lived to see it succeeded and ruled by Cyrus.

It is important to realize that in this introductory story and in all
the stories that follow, the central protagonist and the hero of the
stories is not Daniel nor any of his friends. The main character of
the Book of Daniel is God. He is the living God, utterly unlike the
dead idols and false gods that surrounded Daniel in Babylon. He is
the God who acts, not just in His own land of Israel but in all the
earth, for He is sovereign over all nations. He acted with power in
Palestine when His people lived in His land. He acts with power
in foreign Babylon when His people are sent into exile there. God

is the One occupying center stage throughout all these tales. Daniel and his friends are there to witness to His power and to receive a reward for persevering in their faith, but God remains the hero and the main character. If the stories were made into a movie, God would properly be its star.

This first story has lasting lessons for us, the foremost of which is that God rewards integrity and faithfulness to Him when it is coupled with humility. In this story, Daniel did not cave in to the demands of the idolatrous world around him nor forsake faithfulness to his God. But neither did he take a proud, defiant stand and simply refuse to eat the food provided. Rather, he humbly asked to be allowed to eat an alternative diet, made a suggestion that such a diet be tested, and then left the final decision with his superior. Daniel thus exercised both faithfulness before God and humility before men, and it was this potent combination of virtues that God rewarded. He will reward such virtues in us also as we serve Him in our own secular society.

This opening story also introduces certain themes. It addresses the difference between Jewish religion and paganism, as well as examining the temptation to apostatize from that religion for the sake of cultural advancement, and how God rewards those who remain faithful to Him. As such, this first story sets the tone for all the successive stories found in the first half of the book. Those stories will revisit these themes again and again, showing in the various contests between Daniel and his friends on the one hand and the pagan kings on the other how important it is to remain faithful to God in a hostile pagan world. God has begun to work wonders in the land of exile; He will work many more in the pages to come.

PART 2

The Adventures of Daniel and His Friends at the King's Court

Nebuchadnezzar's Dream

God Reveals His Plan to Set Up an Eternal Kingdom

2 ¹ Now in the second year of the reign of Nebuchadnezzar, Nebuchadnezzar had dreams; and his spirit was troubled, and his sleep left him. ² Then the king said to call the astrologers, the enchanters, the sorcerers, and the Chaldeans to tell the king his dreams. So they came and stood before the king. ³ And the king said to them, "I have had a dream, and my spirit is troubled to know the dream." ⁴ Then the Chaldeans spoke to the king in Aramaic, "O king, live forever! Tell your servants the dream, and we will reveal the interpretation." ⁵ The king answered and said to the Chaldeans, "My word is sure: if you do not make known to me the dream and its interpretation, you shall be cut limb from limb, and your houses shall be made into a dunghill. ⁶ However, if you tell the dream and its interpretation, you shall receive from me gifts, and a reward, and great honor. Therefore tell me the dream and its interpretation." ⁷ They answered again and said, "Let the king tell his servants the dream, and we will reveal its interpretation." ⁸ The king answered and said, "I know for certain that you are trying to gain time, because you see that my word is sure. ⁹ If you do not make known the dream to me, there is only one sentence for you! For you have agreed to speak lying and corrupt words

before me till the times have changed. Therefore tell me the dream, and I shall know that you can reveal to me its interpretation." [10] The Chaldeans answered the king and said, "There is not a man on earth who can tell the king's matter; therefore no king, lord, or ruler has ever asked such things of any enchanter, astrologer, or Chaldean. [11] The thing that the king asks is difficult, and there is no other who can tell it to the king except the gods, whose dwelling is not with flesh." [12] For this reason the king was enraged and angry, and commanded to destroy all the wise men of Babylon. [13] So the sentence went out that the wise men were to be killed; and they sought Daniel and his companions to kill them.

The skillful narrator then switches to another time in the future, a time when Daniel and his companions are well established as members of the Chaldean guild. The present story thus builds on the previous narrative, though without any apparent connective. The change, in fact, is intentionally abrupt, switching from young Daniel at the court to the mighty King Nebuchadnezzar in his royal palace. The change is intended to arouse interest and make the listener sit up. We are at the royal palace, and the king there **had dreams; and his spirit was troubled, and sleep left him.** What dreams? What can it mean? And what could it possibly have to do with Daniel? Astute readers of the tale will remember similar words being spoken when Pharaoh had a dream, the meaning of which Joseph explained (Gen. 41:8). In this way the narrator skillfully prepares us for the coming of Daniel as a new Joseph and friend to the king. We begin to take the first steps into a larger-than-life story.

Once again, however, at the outset of the tale, we meet another historical difficulty regarding dates.[4] The reference here to the

---

4   The story of the king's dream is dated to the second year of Nebuchadnezzar's reign. The earliest Daniel and his companions could have landed in Babylon

second year of Nebuchadnezzar's reign reveals the story to be an historical romance, rather than actual history, and functions to bring to the tale a measure of verisimilitude. But whatever its historicity, the narrator presents Nebuchadnezzar as one who is tormented by dreams in the night, so that after this dream he could find no rest, either in the day (**his spirit was troubled**) or by night (**his sleep left him**). When we learn from the narrative that the dream involved a large statue bearing his own image being suddenly shattered and every trace of it blown away, it could be that the king feared the dream was a portent of future assassination. No wonder he could find no rest.

The king therefore called not simply his regular staff of **astrologers** and **enchanters** (mentioned as his regular staff in 1:20), but also a crew of **sorcerers** and **Chaldeans**. This expanded staff shows the king's desperation to solve the riddle. The term *sorcerer* is a dark one in the Book of Daniel, for it was used of the sorcerers of Pharaoh in Exodus 7:11 and for those practicing abominable sorcery in Deuteronomy 18:10. The term *Chaldean* here refers not to the

---

and been considered for service at the royal court was the third year of King Jehoiakim, dated to 606 BC by Dan. 1:1. As the crown prince of Babylon, Nebuchadnezzar defeated the Egyptians at Carchemish on the Euphrates, forcing them to withdraw. Soon after this his father, the king of Babylon Nabopolassar, died, and Nebuchadnezzar returned to Babylon to become its next king. This was in 605. The second year of his reign, therefore, was 604. Daniel 1:5 says that it took Daniel three years to complete his training, so that the earliest he could have finished his training and been enrolled at court therefore was 603. So the second year of Nebuchadnezzar was a year before Daniel could have been enrolled in his court. Even if adjustment of the year is made by citing the system of not counting the accession year as part of the king's reign, the difficulty remains that Daniel 2:25 says Daniel was unknown to Nebuchadnezzar in the second year of his reign, whereas Daniel 1:20 says that at the end of his three-year training Daniel was known to the king as one who was better than all his professional sages. It appears that the stories of chapters 1 and 2 originally circulated independently of each other.

ethnic people of Chaldea but to a class of professional soothsayers.[5]
We look therefore upon a grand gathering at his royal court of all
who could possibly help the king resolve the matter. The narrator
seems to use the four terms interchangeably to mean "soothsayers of
all sorts" (thus "the Chaldeans" replying in verse 4 refers not to just
the Chaldeans of the group but to the group as a whole).

Not unnaturally, when the king demanded to **know** the meaning of **the dream**, the Chaldeans replied to the king, "**O king, live
forever! Tell your servants the dream, and we will reveal the
interpretation**," for this was the standard practice. To their shock,
the king refused to divulge the dream, but irrationally insisted that
they tell him what he had dreamed as well as what it meant. This
had no precedent in the practice of soothsaying and defied all logic.
Not only that, the king reinforced his demand by threatening to
slaughter all those of the Chaldean caste in his realm if they did
not comply—the offending staff would be **cut limb from limb** and
their **houses made into a dunghill**. To this stick was added a car-
rot: if they did comply, they would **receive gifts, a reward, and
great honor**. The king said "**my word is sure**," using the Persian
loan word *azda*, meaning "publicly proclaimed" and thus "certain."
This was not merely angry rhetoric, but a certainty.

Dumbfounded, the Chaldeans could only repeat their original
request to know the contents of the dream. The king rejected this
request entirely, accusing them of trying to **gain time** and wait till
the times (i.e., the situation) had **changed** and the king forgot or
relented. When they remained adamant that the king was asking
for the impossible and insisted "**there is not a man on earth who**

---

5   Some scholars say that such a usage would have been inconceivable in the
     time of Daniel, when the Chaldeans were a ruling people in the world, and
     such a restricted use of the term dates only from the later Hellenistic period,
     its first extant use being Herodotus (d. 425 BC). Some cite this as evidence
     for a later date of the Book of Daniel.

can tell the king's matter, for **there is no other** who can work such a miracle **except the gods, whose dwelling is not with flesh,**" the king became enraged and ordered the previously threatened slaughter of every professional soothsayer in his land.

This motif can be found in many such court tales. Nebuchadnezzar here looks more like a murderous caricature than an historical figure. The Chaldeans' emphatic and repeated admission of helpless inability to solve the mystery sets the scene for Daniel once again to prove his superiority to them by answering the king.

We note that this entire exchange is reported in Aramaic, for with verse 4 the language of the text changes from Hebrew to Aramaic.[6] Indeed, the narrator introduces the change by saying that after the king demanded to know the meaning of his dream, **the Chaldeans spoke to the king in Aramaic**. The narrator may have thought, on the basis on 2 Kings 18:26, that the Babylonian sages would have most likely spoken to their king in Aramaic, the international *lingua franca* of that time, rather than in the expected Babylonian or Akkadian. Here we simply note that the change of language from Hebrew to Aramaic results in the listener feeling that he has zeroed in on the situation and now occupies a ringside seat. In this exchange between the king and the Chaldeans, the entire priestly caste of mighty Babylon has been reduced to frightened and quivering impotence. So much for the glorious wisdom of the pagans!

[14] Then with prudence and insight Daniel answered Arioch, the chief of the slaughterers, who had gone out to kill the wise men of Babylon; [15] he answered and said to Arioch the

---

6   Scholars have debated whether the Aramaic of the Book of Daniel represents an Aramaic in existence later than that used in the time of the exile, so that its use here is evidence for a Hellenistic date for the book.

king's captain, "Why is the decree from the king so severe?"
Then Arioch made known the matter to Daniel. [16] So Daniel went in and asked from the king that he might give him
time, that he might make known to the king the interpretation. [17] Then Daniel went to his house and made known
the matter to Hananiah, Mishael, and Azariah, his companions, [18] that they might seek mercies from the God of heaven
concerning this secret, so that Daniel and his companions
might not perish with the rest of the wise men of Babylon. [19] Then the secret was revealed to Daniel in a vision of the
night. Then Daniel blessed the God of heaven.

We note that the towering rage of the king and the quivering terror of the Chaldeans serve as a contrast to the calm and measured
serenity of Daniel. One might expect that a Jew, as a recent captive arrival and a stranger in a foreign land, would quake at the
royal threat even more than the established and native professionals
of Babylon, especially when threatened with the same sentence of
slaughter. But in the succeeding narrative Daniel shines as a model
of imperturbable confidence.

Thus instead of fleeing from Arioch,[7] the chief of the guards and
police (lit., **chief of the slaughterers**; the word here should be translated according to its strict etymological meaning rather than its
later meaning), Daniel sought him out and simply asked to know,
"Why is the decree of the king so severe?" His calm and fear-
less confidence contrasts with the panic which we suppose seized
the Chaldeans. Surprisingly (and to reinforce the status Daniel has
acquired with important people like the police chief), instead of

---

7   The name Arioch is found also in Gen. 14:1 as the name of the king of
    Ellasar and in Judith 1:6 as the name of the king of the Elymaeans. It could
    be that the narrator thought it a foreign-enough-sounding name to be used
    here. Or it could be that Arioch is simply a title, meaning "lion."

simply carrying out the king's sentence, Arioch stopped to explain the whole situation to Daniel. Daniel's response to this information again reveals his inner *gravitas* and serenity: instead of running away from the king and hiding, he rather **went in and asked from the king that he might give him time** to learn what the dream was (probably through prayer and fasting). The king was unwilling to accede to any of the requests of his own Chaldean professionals and accused them of playing for time, but here he immediately grants Daniel's request for more time. The narrator thus builds up the contrast between Daniel the Jew and the pagan Chaldeans.

Having been given time, Daniel enlisted the help of his compatriots and in prayer sought **mercies of the God of heaven concerning this** royal **secret**. Though Daniel is supposedly one of the threatened caste of Chaldeans (v. 13), he did not consult with any of them nor ask for their help. Rather he confided in and sought help from his fellow Jews. The lesson is clear: God's holy people must stick together in foreign lands and refuse to rely on pagan help (we note in v. 23 that Daniel uses the singular and the plural interchangeably in his prayer, since he identifies so completely with his compatriots). Of course God hearkened to his prayer, and **the secret was revealed to Daniel in a vision of the night**—that is, not in a normal dream, but in a divine vision.

20 Daniel answered and said:
   "Blessed be the Name of God forever and ever,
   for wisdom and strength belong to Him.
21 And He changes the times and the seasons;
   He removes kings and sets up kings;
   He gives wisdom to the wise
   and knowledge to those who have understanding.
22 He reveals deep and mysterious things;
   He knows what is in the darkness,

and light dwells with Him.
23 To You, O God of my fathers,
   I give thanks and praise,
   for You have given me wisdom and strength,
   and have now made known to me what we asked of You,
   for You have made known to us the king's matter."
24 Therefore Daniel went to Arioch, whom the king had
   appointed to destroy the wise men of Babylon. He went
   and said thus to him, "Do not destroy the wise men of
   Babylon; take me before the king, and I will tell the king the
   interpretation."

The prayer of Daniel that follows is not simply filler; rather, it expresses the beating heart of the book, and its importance is shown by its poetic form. It is the central contention of the Book of Daniel that the pagan rulers do not actually rule the world as they imagine, but the God of Israel accomplishes His purposes through them, and they are merely His instruments. That is why His people can be calm and serene in the tumultuous world, even when persecuted and threatened with slaughterers, fiery furnaces, and ferocious lions. Despite all the backroom deals, political treaties, and secret operations of nations, **wisdom and strength belong to Him**. He alone **changes times and seasons** and regimes; He alone **removes kings and sets up kings. He gives wisdom to the wise**, such as those like Daniel, and to any who **have understanding** enough to retain piety in the face of secular attack. **Darkness** and **light** are alike to Him. He sees all so that no plan or purpose may withstand Him.

Armed with the revelation God gave him, **Daniel went to Arioch** again with a request for another audience (the narrator stresses Daniel's courage by repeating that Arioch was the one **whom the king appointed to destroy the wise men**). Daniel's message is dramatic, and we can almost hear the breathless urgency as the executioner's sword was about to descend upon all the Chaldeans throughout the empire: **"Do not destroy the wise men of Babylon; take me before the king, and I will tell the king the interpretation."** Daniel saves the day. He not only proves himself superior to the Chaldeans because he knows God, but he now functions as their savior too.

²⁵ Then Arioch hurriedly brought Daniel before the king and said thus to him, "I have found a man of the exiles of Judah who will make known to the king the interpretation." ²⁶ The king answered and said to Daniel, whose name was Belteshazzar, "Are you able to make known to me the dream which I have seen and its interpretation?" ²⁷ Daniel answered before the king and said, "The secret which the king has asked, the wise men, the enchanters, the astrologers, and the soothsayers cannot show to the king. ²⁸ But there is a God in heaven who reveals secrets, and He has made known to King Nebuchadnezzar what will be in the latter days. Your dream, and the visions of your head on your bed, were these: ²⁹ as for you, O king, thoughts came while on your bed, about what would come to pass after this; and the Revealer of secrets has made known to you what will be. ³⁰ And as for me, this secret has not been revealed to me because I have more wisdom than any living man, but in order that the interpretation may be made known to the king, and that you may know the thoughts of your heart. ³¹ You, O king, saw, and behold, a great image! That great image, of extraordinary brightness, stood before you; and its appearance was terrifying. ³² That image's head was of fine gold, its breast and arms of silver, its belly and its thighs of bronze. ³³ Its legs were of iron, its feet partly of iron and partly of clay. ³⁴ You continued watching while a stone was cut out without hands, which struck the image on its feet of iron and clay, and crushed them. ³⁵ Then together the iron, the clay, the

bronze, the silver, and the gold were crushed and became like
chaff from the summer threshing floors; the wind carried them
away so that not a trace of them was found. But the stone that
struck the image became a great mountain and filled the whole
earth.

The drama continues as Arioch hurriedly brings Daniel before the
king and introduces him to Nebuchadnezzar, saying, "**I have found
a man of the exiles of Judah who will make known to the king
the interpretation**"—in other words, the king need not enforce his
order to slay all the Chaldeans. We note that in this tale Daniel
seems to be introduced to the king for the first time.[8] The king asks
this newly discovered man if he is able to **make known the dream**
as well as **its interpretation**, despite the fact that the Chaldeans
have declared such a thing impossible for men. Daniel's answer confirms the inability and folly of the pagan **wise men, the enchanters, the astrologers, and the soothsayers**—in other words, the
whole pagan religion of Babylon. (They are grouped together and
enumerated to stress their incompetence.) But he also declares the
power of the Jewish **God in heaven who reveals secrets**. He, Daniel says, has **made known to King Nebuchadnezzar what will be
in latter days**. The true God of heaven knows all, and He has graciously revealed His purposes to the one whom He has placed over
all the earth as the king of kings. With those words, Daniel reveals
to the king what the Chaldeans could not reveal—the dream God
gave to Nebuchadnezzar. In explaining the dream, Daniel is careful

---

8   Even if room is found for Daniel's three-year training before this, so that
     Daniel has just been introduced to the king at the end of his training,
     Arioch's introduction here reads oddly when compared to Daniel 1. In that
     chapter, the king found Daniel to be ten times better than all the other
     Chaldeans. If that were so, why then did the king not consult Daniel before
     this? It looks as if the two stories circulated independently and were brought
     together here by the narrator with little concern for historical consistency.

to stress that the insight comes not from Daniel himself, who has no **more wisdom than any living man**, but from his God, **the Revealer of secrets**. It is His will to share His plans with the king.

With that, Daniel proceeds to narrate the king's dream. With a dramatic and customary[9] **behold!** to stress the shock the king received in his dream, Daniel describes the image the king saw as **great** in size, of **extraordinary brightness**, with a **terrifying appearance**. As if to add to the disjointed weirdness of the vision, the image was not made from a single component but from a mixture of many: its **head was of fine gold**, while **its breast and arms** were **of silver, its belly and its thighs of bronze, its legs were of iron**, and **its feet partly of iron and partly of clay**. Our long familiarity with the Book of Daniel can blind us to the horror of such an image, especially in the eyes of the Jews, for whom mixing was unnatural (compare Deut. 22:9–11, which prohibits sowing one's field with two kinds of seed and wearing clothes of mingled fibers).

The horror of the image's unnatural size, brightness, and composition was increased when Nebuchadnezzar **continued watching** (in terrified fascination), only to see **a stone cut out without hands** which **struck the image on its feet and crushed them**. Then not just the feet (as might be expected), but the entire image was crushed to bits, so that it **became like chaff from the summer threshing floors**. At last **the wind carried them away so that not a trace of them was found**. As a final twist, the supernatural **stone** which brought destruction **became a great mountain and filled the whole earth**. If the king was alarmed at the destructive power brought by such a small stone, his alarm would have increased to terror when he saw such a lethal weapon of annihilation grow and

---

9   Instances of introducing such dreams with "behold!" can be found in Dan. 4:10; 7:2; 8:3; Zech. 1:18; 2:1; 5:1; 6:1.

fill the earth. What other destruction might come next from the terrible stone?

³⁶ "This is the dream; now we will tell the interpretation of it before the king. ³⁷ You, O king, are the king of kings, for the God of heaven has given you the kingdom, the power, the strength, and the glory; ³⁸ and wherever they dwell, the sons of men, the beasts of the field and the birds of the air, He has given them into your hand, making you rule over them all— you are that head of gold. ³⁹ But after you shall arise another kingdom inferior to yours; then another, a third kingdom of bronze, which shall rule in all the earth. ⁴⁰ And there shall be a fourth kingdom, as strong as iron, because iron crushes and smashes all things; and like iron that shatters, that kingdom will crush and shatter all these. ⁴¹ And as you saw the feet and toes, partly of potter's clay and partly of iron, that kingdom shall be divided; yet the firmness of the iron shall be in it, just as you saw the iron mixed with ceramic clay. ⁴² And as the toes of the feet were partly of iron and partly of clay, so the kingdom shall be partly strong and partly brittle. ⁴³ As you saw iron mixed with ceramic clay, they will mingle with the seed of men; but they will not adhere to one another, just as iron does not mix with clay. ⁴⁴ And in the days of these kings, the God of heaven will set up a kingdom which shall never be destroyed; and the kingdom shall not be left to another people; it shall crush all these kingdoms and finish them, and it shall stand forever. ⁴⁵ Just as you saw that the stone was cut out from the mountain without hands, and that it crushed the iron, the bronze, the clay, the silver, and the gold—the great God has made known to the king what will happen hereafter. The dream is certain, and its interpretation is sure."

Having correctly described the king's dream and assured him of his divine ability, Daniel went on to explain its meaning. Daniel began by examining the terrifying image from the top down, pointedly saying to Nebuchadnezzar, **"You, O king, are the king of kings."** This fact should not cause the king to puff himself up with fatal hubris, for his supremacy is the gift of the **God of heaven,** who has exalted him over all the world. Though Daniel does not take pains to say so, the reader is expected to identify this "God of heaven" with the Jewish God of Daniel, even though a Babylonian such as Nebuchadnezzar would have identified him with Marduk (or Bel), head of the Babylonian pantheon. Since God has exalted Nebuchadnezzar to rule over all the earth, he is obviously **the head of gold**.

As well as explaining the dream, Daniel's emphasis on the king's vast and universal authority has the effect of flattery, which kings came to expect of those addressing them. In learning that Nebuchadnezzar was the head of gold, one might conclude also that the facial features of the image were those of Nebuchadnezzar, and doubtless this is why its destruction by the lethal stone caused him such anxiety.

Daniel deals with the next features of the statue more summarily. He almost skips over them, saying that **"after you shall arise another kingdom inferior to yours,"** symbolized by the breast and arms of silver, and **"then another, a third kingdom of bronze,"** which despite its position as third on the image **shall rule in all the earth**. These kingdoms have no important place in Daniel's interpretation here. He places greater stress on the **fourth kingdom**, which shall be **strong as iron**, because just like iron, which can **crush and smash all things, that kingdom will** also **crush and shatter all these** other kingdoms. Yet for all its might, it has a hidden fragility, an inner weakness, for the **kingdom shall be divided** and thus politically unstable. Iron does not mix with clay, and so as the king **saw iron mixed with ceramic clay**, this kingdom **will mingle with the seed of men**, trying to shore itself up and find unity through marriage alliances among its rulers. The mighty iron kingdom will contain its own weakness.[10]

The vision then reaches its climax. In the coming days that were shown to the king, **the God of heaven** will **set up a kingdom which shall never be destroyed**, one that will replace these kingdoms and will itself never be replaced. That is what **the stone cut out from the mountain without hands** means—this kingdom will not be established by human might but solely by the supernatural power of God. And this kingdom, though initially as small as a stone, will grow and **fill the whole earth**, leaving no room for any other kingdom. Nebuchadnezzar thus stands at the head of a line of human empires that will give place to the rule of the God of heaven forever. It is a sign of divine favor to the king that **God made known what will happen hereafter**. There is nothing anyone can do to change the rise and fall of the kingdoms that will succeed Nebuchadnezzar's Babylon, nor to impede the coming rule of God's kingdom. The future is inalterably set;[11] **the dream is certain, and its interpretation is sure**.

What does it all mean? In terms of the narrative, it means the king is in no danger of assassination—or, at least, the dream is not an omen of it. That is why in the story Nebuchadnezzar receives Daniel's interpretation as good news. Babylon will endure and at length be replaced by another kingdom, as all kingdoms rise and

---

10   The historical fulfillment of this detail and the identity of the fourth kingdom will be discussed later.

11   Apocalyptic visions characteristically differ in this way from prophecy: prophecy leaves room for human response and divine changes of plan (see Jonah 2:4; 3:10); apocalyptic revelations do not.

fall.[12] But its glory will never be equaled or surpassed. The next kingdom will be inferior to it (v. 39). The only lasting kingdom will be the kingdom of the God of heaven Himself.

The idea of kingdoms succeeding each other with greater inferiority was not original to this story of the king's dream but was well known in the ancient world. It is reflected, for example, by Hesiod in his *Works and Days*, written sometime between 750 and 650 BC. In this work, Hesiod divided all human history into five eras, four of which are characterized in sequence by metals of gold, silver, bronze, and iron. (Between the last two he inserts the age of Greek heroes.) Thus, in his view, kingdom succeeds kingdom, with each one becoming inferior to its predecessor.

The idea of summing up all history in a list of four successive kingdoms was also common in the ancient world. One finds this idea in the utterances of the fourth Sibyl, a Jewish apocalyptic work using prior material dated to about 140 BC. The female oracle called the Sibyl spoke about all the empires of history as four in number: the Assyrians, the Medes, the Persians, and the Macedonians. Herodotus (d. 425 BC) also wrote about the Assyrians, the Medes, and the Persians as three successive empires, with the Greeks of course inheriting all that came before.

As we read this story of the king's dream, we must not read back into it information from later chapters. In chapter seven, for example, we will hear again of four empires and gain more information that will help us to identify which empires are symbolized by the parts of the statue. But chapter two must be understood on its own.

---

12 The king's satisfaction with Daniel's interpretation shows that we should interpret the succeeding kings as kingdoms, and not as Nebuchadnezzar's immediate Babylonian successors, Amel-Marduk, Neriglissar and Nabonidus, as some have suggested. It is difficult to imagine that Nebuchadnezzar would have taken much satisfaction in learning that his dynasty was about to get wiped out.

Here the identification of the four empires is not very important; the only important things are the glory of Nebuchadnezzar and the final annihilation of all earthly empires when God's kingdom finally comes. The identity of the future empires with their many historical details only gradually comes into focus throughout the Book of Daniel. We will look again at the succession of empires in later chapters, as the narrator repeatedly focuses upon them. Here he is concerned only with the certainty of God's eventual triumph.

> [46] Then King Nebuchadnezzar fell on his face and worshiped Daniel, and commanded that a grain offering and incense be offered to him. [47] The king answered Daniel and said, "Truly your God is God of gods and Lord of kings, and a revealer of secrets, since you were able to reveal this secret." [48] Then the king exalted Daniel and gave him many great gifts; and he made him ruler over the whole province of Babylon and chief prefect over all the wise men of Babylon. [49] Also Daniel asked the king, and he appointed Shadrach, Meshach, and Abed-Nego over the affairs of the province of Babylon; but Daniel sat in the gate of the king.

Like the beginning of the tale, the conclusion reads larger than life. When the story began, the king acted in a murderously perverse way, with the genocidal fury that belongs to historical romances rather than to history. In the same way, the king at the conclusion acts with a generosity that matches his previous fury. Moreover, his response toward Daniel also reads like an historical romance. Gifts, honors, and political promotion such as he bestows upon the unknown seer might have been expected, but no one could guess that the great ruler of the world would **fall on his face and worship Daniel**, the previously unknown refugee, only lately come to court.

Here the narrator expects the listener to take polemical

satisfaction at the spectacle of the mighty king abasing himself before one of his captives. The king does not just acknowledge the God of the Jews, but even worships a Jew! That this worship was the intention of the king's action (rather than a simple act of prostration—though this in itself would be astounding) is apparent from his next command, for Nebuchadnezzar orders that **a grain offering and incense be offered to him**—the very gifts offered to a deity.[13] The word rendered "grain offering" is *minchah*, the usual term for a food offering to God (e.g., Lev. 2:1f); the use of incense also formed an invariable part of sacrifices to God (e.g., Ex. 40:27). And the king makes a very Jewish confession, praising Daniel's God as **God of gods and Lord of kings**. One would think the pagan king had become a Jew—were it not for his worship of Daniel.

The story ends with the king promoting Daniel to a high position as **chief prefect over all the wise men of Babylon** (i.e., as head over the caste of Chaldeans[14]), and with Daniel also securing the promotion of his threatened compatriots (v. 13) so they too

13 Some try to blunt the significance of the king's prostration by citing Josephus' story (*Antiquities* 11, 8, 5) of Alexander the Great's famous prostration to the Jewish high priest, for Alexander then explained that the prostration was not meant as adoration of the priest but only as an honor directed to the God who gave him the high priesthood. Alexander's prostration is not really a parallel, for the prostration of Nebuchadnezzar is but one part of an entire story containing fantastic improbabilities. Some have objected that pious Daniel would never have accepted such worship; but the narrator was not here concerned with Daniel, but solely with the satisfaction provided to the hearer by the spectacle of a heathen king thus bowing before one of their own. Besides, even in the tale itself, if the murderous king wanted to worship Daniel, what could he sensibly do but receive it meekly?

14 Thus in 4:9 Daniel is identified as the "chief of the astrologers"—i.e., as functioning head of the Chaldean priestly caste. How this harmonizes with Daniel's previous determination to avoid such Chaldean contamination (1:8, 16) is difficult to imagine. This is further evidence that the two stories in chapters 1 and 2 originally circulated independently of each other.

could enjoy safety. Meanwhile Daniel himself remained at the capital, **in the gate of the king**—at the king's royal court, waiting for his command. With these jaw-dropping acts of Nebuchadnezzar, the narrator sets the scene for the crisis narrated in the next chapter.

WHEN WE HEAR THIS STORY AS THE NARRATOR INTENDED, we find a series of wonders. The tale opens with a king vexed with a disturbing dream. Next comes the spectacle of a gathering of all the sages, professionals, and insightful men with long experience in interpreting such dreams. But to our surprise, the king refuses to divulge his dream to them and yet demands that they declare both its content and its interpretation. More amazing still, he threatens all the men standing before him, as well as all the sages like them throughout his realm, with death and the ruination of their families if they do not immediately comply with his demand. Clearly, the king has turned into a madman.

As the terrible sentence is being carried out, Daniel is discovered in obscurity by one of the king's agents, who allows him time to seek for God's help. God grants a miraculous vision to Daniel, who is quickly hustled into the king's presence. Daniel immediately discloses both the dream and its meaning. The murderous king has a complete and astounding *volte-face* and prostrates himself before Daniel in worship, ordering that he be given other divine honors. Daniel is promoted as head over all the other sages and succeeds in getting his friends promoted too. The story is thrilling, and hearing it is like riding a literary roller coaster. Historical questions should not be allowed to push aside this fundamental fact that the Word of God contains such a heart-pounding and wonderful story.

But what does it mean for us? The story of Nebuchadnezzar's dream and its interpretation teaches several lessons of lasting value.

First of all, it shows that God's people should not be overly impressed by the glory of the world, with its dazzling parade of wealth and celebrity. The Chaldeans of this age may look impressive, but in reality they are useless and retain no lasting glory. The worldling is powerless and quivering in the face of death, whatever his earthly splendor.

Secondly, this story shows that God's people need fear nothing from the world. Daniel did not quake in fear or flee when threatened but remained calm, trusting in God. Since he knew God, he had access to a wisdom and strength not available to the world (v. 23), and this was the hidden source of his serenity.

Finally, this tale shows that eventually the world will give place to the eternal Kingdom of God. The matter is sure (v. 45), and the apocalypticists were right: God will triumph, and there is nothing anyone can do about it. In this certainty we can find our peace, even in a strange land.

DANIEL 3

Nebuchadnezzar's Furnace

God Rescues His Faithful Ones When They Defy Idolatry

3 ¹ King Nebuchadnezzar made an image of gold; its height was sixty cubits and its width six cubits. He set it up on the plain of Dura, in the province of Babylon. ² Then King Nebuchadnezzar sent to assemble the satraps, the prefects, the governors, the counselors, the treasurers, the judges, the magistrates, and all the officials of the provinces, to come to the dedication of the image which King Nebuchadnezzar had set up. ³ So the satraps, the prefects, the governors, the counselors, the treasurers, the judges, the magistrates, and all the officials of the provinces assembled for the dedication of the image that King Nebuchadnezzar had set up; and they stood before the image that Nebuchadnezzar had set up. ⁴ Then a herald shouted aloud: "To you it is commanded, O peoples, nations, and languages, ⁵ that at the time you hear the sound of the horn, flute, lyre, harp, psaltery, and drum with all kinds of music, you shall fall down and worship the golden image that King Nebuchadnezzar has set up; ⁶ and whoever does not fall down and worship shall immediately be cast into the midst of a burning fiery furnace!" ⁷ So at that time, when all the people heard the sound of the horn, flute, lyre, harp, and psaltery with all kinds of music, all the people, nations, and languages

fell down and worshiped the golden image which King Nebuchadnezzar had set up. [8] Therefore at that time certain Chaldeans came forward and slandered the Jews. [9] They spoke and
said to King Nebuchadnezzar, "O king, live forever! [10] You, O
king, have made a decree that every man who hears the sound
of the horn, flute, lyre, harp, psaltery, and drum with all kinds
of music, shall fall down and worship the golden image; [11] and
whoever does not fall down and worship shall be cast into the
midst of a burning fiery furnace. [12] There are certain Jews whom
you have appointed over the affairs of the province of Babylon:
Shadrach, Meshach, and Abed-Nego; these men, O king, pay
no heed to you. They do not serve your gods or worship the
golden image which you have set up."

The next story is not dated,[15] but it presupposes the promotions of
Shadrach, Meshach, and Abed-Nego **over the affairs of the province of Babylon**—that is, it belongs to a time after Nebuchadnezzar had been so impressed with Daniel and his God in chapter two
and had promoted his friends. Like the last tale, this one focuses
upon **King Nebuchadnezzar. He made an image of gold; its
height was sixty cubits and its width six cubits**. There is no suggestion in the text that it was an image of himself, and the statement of verse 12 that the Jews do **not serve your gods or worship
the golden image which you have set up** suggests that the image
was of Nebuchadnezzar's god, probably Bel/Marduk, the head of
the Babylonian pantheon.

Such images were by no means unheard of in paganism. Herodotus (*History* 1.183) reports a "sitting figure of Zeus, all of gold" in
the Babylonian temple of Bel, and "a figure of a man, twelve cubits
high, entirely of solid gold" in the same temple. This image dwarfed

---

15   The Greek versions date this to Nebuchadnezzar's eighteenth year—i.e., to
     the year of the fall of Jerusalem.

them all: being **sixty cubits** high, it stood ninety feet tall—twice the height of Solomon's temple (1 Kin. 6:2), with only the Colossus of Rhodes, one of the Seven Wonders of the World, standing taller at seventy cubits. Freakishly, **its width** was only **six cubits**, or nine feet. The whole description of the image is meant to evoke not just wonder, but horror; the monstrosity stood against the sky like a freak, a divine provocation. It was **set up on the plain of Dura**—that is, probably on the flat outside the city wall (from the Akkadian *duru*, "walled place, fortification").

At the time of its dedication, **King Nebuchadnezzar sent to assemble** all rulers and officials, that their assembled pomp might honor the god whose image had been erected. The enumeration of them as **the satraps, the prefects, the governors, the counselors, the treasurers, the judges, the magistrates,**[16] **and all the officials of the provinces** is satirical, as the narrator mocks the useless proliferation of pagan bureaucrats. When the appropriate time came, a herald shouted aloud, **"To you it is commanded, O peoples, nations, and languages, that at the time you hear the sound of the horn, flute, lyre, harp, psaltery, and drum with all kinds of music, you shall fall down and worship the gold image that King Nebuchadnezzar has set up,**[17] **and whoever does not fall down and worship shall immediately be cast into the midst of a burning fiery furnace!"**

The public command was extraordinary. The narrator portrays it in all its self-important, unnecessary, and ridiculous pomp (**O peoples, nations, and languages**). He also stresses the ridiculousness of the command by repeatedly listing all the musical instruments.

---

16   Most of the titles are Medo-Persian or Persian in origin, suggesting a time later than Nebuchadnezzar.

17   The repetition of the phrase "which he had set up" (in vv. 2, 3, 5, 7, 12, 14, 18) is part of the satire.

But even more extraordinary is the sanction for disobedience—whoever refuses to worship will be cast alive into a fiery furnace! Such a sanction for failure to worship is undocumented in the ancient world until the persecution of Antiochus Epiphanes in the second century B.C. Why would the king, in that polytheistic culture, care if someone didn't worship his gods? It was axiomatic then that everyone worshipped whatever god they chose. And why would he assume that someone would refuse and include the unheard-of sanction for refusal in the proclamation itself? And why such severe punishment?—not just execution, but execution in such a barbaric way, and with such urgency (**shall *immediately* be cast**)? All these details build up a picture of Nebuchadnezzar as a deranged madman (a picture consistent with the unreasonable demands and fury described in the previous chapter).

Regarding those musical instruments: as mentioned above, the narrator lists the instruments and repeats the list again and again in the text in order to make the pagan oppressors look ridiculous. But scholars have long puzzled over exactly what instruments are meant, and complete certainty is elusive. The **horn** (*qeren*) is clearly a kind of cornet or trumpet. The word rendered here **flute** is *mashroqi*, possibly cognate with the Hebrew word "to hiss," suggesting the sound of a flute or perhaps a double pipe. The word here rendered **lyre** is *qitaros*. In the Greek version of Daniel, it is translated *kitharis* (from which we get the modern word "guitar"). The word translated here **harp** is the Aramaic *sabk*, possibly a four-stringed triangular harp. The word rendered here **psaltery** is from *pesanterin*, itself a translation of the Greek *psalterion*, another stringed instrument. Even less certainty attaches to the last word in the list, *sumponyah*, clearly from the Greek *symphonia* (lit., "accompanying sound").[18]

---

18   Some scholars suggest that the terms *pesanterin* and *sumponyah*, being based on much later Greek words (*psalterion* is found in Aristotle, d. 322, and

Some have suggested it means "bagpipe"; others, that it refers not to a musical instrument at all but to the practice of playing all the instruments in unison. Some have suggested that it should be translated as **drum**, which we have chosen for our translation here.

Given the threat attached to the royal command, it is not surprising that **all the people, nations, and languages fell down and worshiped the golden image which King Nebuchadnezzar set up**. As pagans they would have no reason not to worship another pagan god, and they had every reason to fear the wrath of the clearly homicidal king. The narrator again subtly satirizes their obedience and pagan religion in general when he lists at length in verse 7 all the musical instruments that summoned them to worship.

This public dedication provided the opportunity for **certain Chaldeans** (members of the priestly caste motivated by jealousy at the recent promotion of the foreigners?) to **slander the Jews**. Under a pretense of concern for the king's honor, **they spoke to King Nebuchadnezzar**, reminding him of his **decree**. They cite the absurd decree in full, including once again a full listing of the musical instruments. (The narrator here is clearly enjoying the satiric barb.) Then they come to the point: **there are certain Jews[19] whom you have appointed over the affairs of the province of Babylon**. Yet despite this gracious royal gift of promoting them to such lofty and important positions, **these men pay** the king **no heed** at all, for **they do not serve** his **gods or worship the golden image** that he

---

symphonia in Plato, d. 348), attest to a late date for the Book of Daniel.

19   The use of the term "Jew" here is anachronistic, pointing to a later date than the exile, for the term "Jew" as a synonym for "Israelite" only became current after the exile. After the exile the Israelites returning from Babylon were called "Jews" regardless of whether or not they were from the tribe of Judah, because they occupied the old territory of Judah. In the Book of Daniel the term indicates someone whose religion is Judaism, not someone from the tribe of Judah. We see the same usage in the Book of Esther: Mordecai is a Jew, even though he is from the tribe of Benjamin (Esth. 3:4; 2:5).

set up. Clearly they are both ungrateful to the king and criminally disobedient to his decree and law.

The stage is set for the showdown between the king and his foreign governors, Shadrach, Meshach, and Abed-Nego, and between power and faith. Given Nebuchadnezzar's irrationally murderous decree and his past behavior, there can be little doubt of the king's reaction to the report of the Chaldeans.

[13] Then Nebuchadnezzar, in anger and fury, commanded to bring Shadrach, Meshach, and Abed-Nego. So they brought these men before the king. [14] Nebuchadnezzar spoke, saying to them, "Is it true, Shadrach, Meshach, and Abed-Nego, that you do not serve my gods or worship the golden image which I have set up? [15] Now if you are ready at the time you hear the sound of the horn, flute, lyre, harp, psaltery, and drum with all kinds of music, and you fall down and worship the image which I have made, good! But if you do not worship, you shall immediately be cast into the midst of a burning fiery furnace. And who is the god that will deliver you from my hands?" [16] Shadrach, Meshach, and Abed-Nego answered and said to the king, "O Nebuchadnezzar, we have no need to answer you in this matter. [17] If there is a God able to deliver us, such as our God whom we serve, He will deliver us from the burning fiery furnace, and from your hand, O king. [18] But if not, let it be known to you, O king, that we will not serve your gods, nor will we worship the golden image which you have set up." [19] Then Nebuchadnezzar was full of fury, and the expression on his face changed toward Shadrach, Meshach, and Abed-Nego. He spoke and ordered to heat the furnace seven times more than it was usually heated. [20] And he ordered certain mighty men of valor of his army to bind Shadrach, Meshach, and Abed-Nego and cast them into the burning fiery furnace. [21] Then these men were bound in their coats, their trousers, their headgear, and

their other garments, and were cast into the midst of the burning fiery furnace. [22] Therefore, because the king's order was strict and the furnace very hot, the flame of the fire killed those men who took up Shadrach, Meshach, and Abed-Nego. [23] And these three men, Shadrach, Meshach, and Abed-Nego, fell bound into the midst of the burning fiery furnace.

Predictably, the king **in anger and fury** commanded his men to bring Shadrach, Meshach, and Abed-Nego before him. With a show of justice and clemency, he gives his erring subjects a chance to repent and do better: can it really be **true** that they **do not serve** his **gods or worship the golden image?** The king is not unreasonable; **if** they are **ready** at the time they hear the music (again the whole orchestra is listed in v. 15; it has become a kind of running joke in the narrative), then all will be well. But **if** they **do not worship**, the sentence will be carried out, and they will **immediately be cast into the midst of a burning fiery furnace**. Then the king asks the question that lies at the heart of the whole Book of Daniel: **"And who is the god that will deliver you from my hands?"** The king is certain that he is supreme over all, including the God of the Jews. Is their God really able to deliver them? Should they not therefore choose capitulation to the all-powerful state over fatal faithfulness to God?

The three youths return a bold and defiant response. They do not begin their reply to Nebuchadnezzar with the customary opening, "O king, live forever!" (compare v. 9). Instead they declare that there is no need to **answer** the king at all in **this matter** of granting a reprieve as a reward for compliance, for such compliance is impossible. And he is wrong about their God too: **"If there is a God able to deliver us, such as our God whom we serve, He will deliver us from the burning fiery furnace, and your hand, O king."** But even **if** their God does **not** deliver them, let the king know for certain that they will **not serve** his **gods nor worship** the **golden image**. Their decision is firm, their defiant refusal of idolatry total.

Predictably, the king was **full of fury**, so much so that his **face** contorted with rage as he ordered his men to **heat the furnace seven times more than it was usually heated**. This command was simply an expression of his rage, since heating the furnace further could not make it more lethal than it already was. Nebuchadnezzar had been furious enough when first informed of the Jews' refusal (v. 13); he was even more furious now. The pointless command to increase the furnace's heat contributes to the picture of Nebuchadnezzar's demented homicidal hysteria.

The shape of the furnace is a matter of scholarly dispute. Some have suggested it was in the shape of a large lime kiln, with a vertical shaft and an opening at the bottom for removing the lime. In the story, the furnace had a large hole at the top (for smoke to ascend and the bodies of victims to descend), as well as a door at the bottom (through which Nebuchadnezzar saw the three youths after they fell to the bottom).

Whatever its shape, the three youths were hustled up to the top of the furnace by the king's men and **cast into the midst of the burning fiery furnace**. Such was the king's wrath that he could not wait until other ropes were found for them. Rather they were **bound** in their own clothes of **coats, trousers, headgear,** and **other garments**. Whatever they were wearing sufficed to bind them. The murderous tyrant could not wait another minute. As if to emphasize the certainty of their doom, the narrator says that the **furnace** was by then so **hot** that **the flame of the fire killed those men** who threw the youths in, despite the fact that they were **mighty men of valor**.

[24] Then King Nebuchadnezzar was astonished and rose in haste and answered and said to his counselors, "Did we

not cast three men bound into the midst of the fire?" They answered and said to the king, "True, O king." ²⁵ "Look!" he answered and said, "I see four men, loose, walking in the midst of the fire; and they are not hurt, and the appearance of the fourth is like a son of the gods!" ²⁶ Then Nebuchadnezzar went near to the door of the burning fiery furnace and answered and said, "Shadrach, Meshach, and Abed-Nego, servants of the Most High God, come out, and come here!" Then Shadrach, Meshach, and Abed-Nego came out from the midst of the fire. ²⁷ And the satraps, prefects, governors, and the king's counselors gathered together, and they saw that the fire had no power over the bodies of those men; the hair of their head was not singed, nor were their garments affected, and the smell of fire did not cling to them. ²⁸ Nebuchadnezzar spoke, saying, "Blessed be the God of Shadrach, Meshach, and Abed-Nego, who sent His angel and delivered His servants who trusted in Him, and they have defied the king's word and given up their bodies, that they should not serve nor worship any god except their own God! ²⁹ And by me a decree is given that any people, nation, or language which speaks anything amiss against the God of Shadrach, Meshach, and Abed-Nego shall be cut limb from limb, and his house shall be made into a dunghill; because there is not another God who can deliver like this!" ³⁰ Then the king promoted Shadrach, Meshach, and Abed-Nego in the province of Babylon.

The story now reaches its miraculous climax. Rather than state what happened to the youths, the narrator skillfully shifts the scene away from the apparently doomed youths back to the king. Throughout the narrative the king appears in his sovereign invincibility—he commands, and his command is carried out, however absurd and irrational it may be. But here we see the king shaken and shocked. He was **astonished and rose in haste**, unable to contain himself and stay seated. He turned to **his counselors** standing by. We can almost see him rub his eyes and splutter to them, "**Did we not cast three men bound into the midst of the fire?**"

The counselors share his pompous confidence, since they evidently did not yet see what their king saw. "**True, O king,**" they replied, possibly with upturned noses. "**Look!**" the king responded, pointing wildly at the door of the furnace. "**I see four men, loose, walking in the midst of the fire; and they are not hurt, and the appearance of the fourth is like a son of the gods!**" Everything is wrong, everything has gone topsy-turvy: not three men, but four! Not bound, but loose! Not dying or dead, but walking around! And the fourth—he shines like a son of the gods! The king's baffled shock is the satisfying climax for the Jewish listener to the story, who instantly sees what Nebuchadnezzar cannot—the hand of the God of Israel, vindicating His servants.

The description in verse 25 of the fourth being in the fire as **like a son of the gods** has, over the years, proven too good a proof text for Christian interpreters to resist, so that the Authorized Version, for example, translated it "the Son of God." In what sense we may interpret the detail christologically will be examined later. Here we simply note that the Aramaic actually reads, *bar elahin*. The *elahin* is plural, and while it is admissible to read the Hebrew plural *elohim* in the singular as "God," the Aramaic plural must be read as a true plural—that is, "gods," members of a divine pantheon. This accords with what a pagan king like Nebuchadnezzar would conclude. The text itself confirms that the fourth being was not God, but simply **His angel** (v. 28)—a conclusion with which a Jewish reader would have agreed, and which is reflected in verse 49 LXX: "the angel of the Lord came down into the furnace." (This is also the opinion of St. Jerome, who wrote in his commentary on Daniel, "I do not know how an ungodly king could have merited a vision of the Son of God. . . . We are to think of angels here." He did allow, however, that it "foreshadows the Lord Jesus.")

Then **Nebuchadnezzar went near the door** and called to them to **come out** and **come here**. But the shocking vision of the divine deliverance changed him—no longer did he regard them as disloyal criminals worthy of a horrible death, but as **servants of the Most High God**. The final proof of God's supremacy overall (and that His servants were right to refuse idolatry) was what all the **satraps, prefects, governors, and counselors** saw when they gathered around them: to their astonishment, **the fire had no power over the bodies of those men; the hair of their head was not singed, nor their garments affected** (i.e., scorched), and not even **the smell of fire** could be detected on them. As the Church would later sing and declare, when God so wills, the order of nature is overturned.

In this catalogue of wonders, we should take special note of the word **power**, for the Book of Daniel is all about power. It might seem as if Nebuchadnezzar, like tyrants before and after him, had all the power, but all the true power belongs to God. He can make His servants powerful if He so wills—more powerful than tyrants and more powerful than fire—even more powerful than death. Little wonder that such an exercise of power compelled the mighty Nebuchadnezzar to exclaim, **"Blessed be the God of Shadrach, Meshach, and Abed-Nego!"** Just like in the end of chapter two (2:47), the pagan king spoke like a good Jewish theologian, declaring that God had **sent His angel and delivered His servants who trusted in Him**. He now saw that they were right to defy **the king's word** even to the point of giving **up their bodies** to death in order **not** to **serve** or **worship** any god except their own God. The Maccabees couldn't have said it better.

The story ends with a typical bit of mocking humor. Ever true to form, the tyrant issues another tyrannical **decree**—but this time in favor of the Jewish religion: **any people, nation, or language which speaks anything amiss against the God of Shadrach, Meshach, and Abed-Nego shall be cut limb from limb, and his house made into a dunghill.** The wording is almost identical to that of 2:5, where Nebuchadnezzar threatened the Chaldeans. *Plus ça change . . .* In this decree the narrator invites the hearer to disdain the pagan power that could be so blundering and blind. The final stroke comes with a career promotion for Shadrach, Meshach, and Abed-Nego.

IF THE STORY OF NEBUCHADNEZZAR'S DREAM INCREASED the element of wonder found in the introductory tale, the story of the fiery furnace increases it even more. This tale begins with a wonder set up in the plain—an architectural freak that somehow embodies all that is unnatural and unnerving about pagan idolatry. Then the king demands that everyone bow down to worship it, adding that refusal will result in immediate execution in the most barbaric way possible. No reason is given for such an astounding sanction.

And when Daniel's friends, lately promoted by him over the affairs of the province of Babylon, refuse, the king goes wild. The king makes no real examination of them to discover the reason for their reluctance. He has no apparent memory of the wonderful revelation made by Daniel, which caused the king to praise his God as "God of gods and Lord of kings" (2:47). The king has seemingly forgotten Daniel and his friends.[20] His inexplicable amnesia has produced a kind of homicidal mania in him, which drives him to

---

20 Also odd is Daniel's absence throughout the whole story. Why did not Daniel have to worship the image along with his friends? Why did he not intercede for them when they were slandered and under threat? These questions of course presuppose that one is reading actual history.

heat the furnace so hot that it even slays the soldiers throwing the Jewish youths into it.

Then (in the original text) comes the climax, with a miracle even greater than Daniel's receiving his revelation in the nick of time: an angel descends into the furnace along with the youths, protecting them from all harm. As with the last story, Nebuchadnezzar the pagan king has yet another *volte-face* and glorifies the God of the Jews. Could the stories of Daniel and his friends witness any greater wonders? Yes: in the very next chapter.

From this chapter we learn a lesson central to the Book of Daniel, and indeed central to the life of God's people in all ages (which is why verses from these chapters figure so prominently in Orthodox hymnography): In every age powerful men will appear, by turns cajoling or threatening, never ceasing until they have worn down the saints and compelled them to surrender their principles. Sometimes they threaten our prosperity or popularity. Sometimes they threaten life itself. These powerful men do not appear pathetic or ridiculous, but suave, sophisticated, enlightened, and reasonable, and for this reason they can be very persuasive.

This story pulls the mask from them and reveals them all to be modern versions of Nebuchadnezzar—raging fools, pathetic indeed in the eyes of heaven. The satire and mockery of Nebuchadnezzar is not merely ancient polemic aimed at a long-dead foe. It is the vigorous spirit and defiance we need today as we face our own secular tyrannies; it is the antidote to cultural poison. Nebuchadnezzar invites mockery—as does the secularism of our times. We must never give in to the spirit of the age but must keep our faith to our dying breath, even if it costs us our life. Whatever fires we must endure, God will send us rescue. In the story, the rescue came from one like a son of the gods. In our life, rescue comes from the Son of God Himself.

ADDITIONS TO THE BOOK OF DANIEL

The Prayer of Azariah and the Hymn of the Three Young Men

The Prayer of Azariah

24 But they walked about in the midst of the fire, praising God and blessing the Lord.

25 Then Azariah stood and prayed thus; in the midst of the fire he opened his mouth and said:

26 "Blessed are You, O Lord, God of our fathers, and worthy of praise;
and glorified is Your Name forever.

27 For You are righteous in all Your deeds,
and true in all Your works and Your ways are upright,
and all Your judgments are true.

28 You have executed true judgments in all that You have brought upon us
and upon Jerusalem, the holy city of our fathers,
for in truth and judgment You have brought all this upon us because of our sins.

29 For we have sinned and broken Your Law in turning from You,
and have sinned in all things and have not obeyed Your commandments.

30 We have not kept them or done them,
as You have commanded us that it might go well with us.

31 So all that You have brought upon us,

and all that You have done to us,
You have done in true judgment.

32 You have given us into the hands of lawless enemies, most
hateful rebels,
and to an unjust king, the most wicked in the world.

33 And now we cannot open our mouth;
shame and disgrace have befallen Your servants and those who
worship You.

34 For Your Name's sake do not give us up utterly,
and do not break Your covenant.

35 Do not withdraw Your mercy from us,
for the sake of Abraham Your beloved
and for the sake of Isaac Your servant
and Israel Your holy one,

36 to whom You promised
to make their descendants as many as the stars of heaven
and as the sand on the seashore.

37 For we, O Master, have become fewer than any nation,
and are brought low this day in all the earth because of our sins.

38 And at this time there is no prince, no prophet, and no leader,
no burnt offering, or sacrifice, or oblation, or incense,
no place to make an offering before You or to find mercy.

39 Yet with a contrite heart and a humble spirit may we be
accepted,
as though it were with burnt offerings of rams and bulls,
and with tens of thousands of fatted lambs;

40 such may our sacrifice be before You this day,
and may we wholly follow You,
for no shame will come to those who trust in You.

41 And now with all our heart we follow,
we fear You and seek Your face.

42 Do not put us to shame,
but deal with us in Your kindness

and in Your abundant mercy.
43 Deliver us by Your marvelous works,
and give glory to Your Name, O Lord!
Let all who do harm to Your servants be put to shame;
let them be disgraced and deprived of all power and dominion,
and let their strength be crushed.
44 Let them know that You alone are the Lord,
and glorious over all the earth."

The Greek version of the Book of Daniel inserts here a long prayer offered by Azariah, one of the three young men. The prayer represents a liturgical lament over the sins that led to Israel's exile, expressing repentance and proclaiming God's justice in His dealings with Israel and Jerusalem (not unlike similar prayers found in Daniel 9:3f and Ezra 9:6f). Azariah prays to God, **"deal with us in Your kindness"** and **"deliver us by Your marvelous works"** (Dan. 3:42–43)—an odd prayer for him to pray at the time when God had in fact just dealt with them according to His kindness and delivered them by His wondrous works from the fiery furnace. Evidently the prayer was written independently of the story and inserted into it with no regard for the flow of the narrative. The one inserting the prayer attempted to link to the story by adding, **But they walked about in the midst of the fire, praising God and blessing the Lord. Then Azariah stood and prayed thus; in the midst of the fire he opened his mouth and said**, but the prayer, wonderful though it may be as a liturgical expression of national contrition, is clearly out of place in the narrative.

The prayer deserves to be considered on its own, for it opens a door into the heart of exiled Israel. Israel had just been soundly beaten by the Babylonians. First the invaders came in 598 BC and deported some of their best and brightest. Then they returned to besiege the city again, and it fell in 587, its king blinded and its temple destroyed. They were tempted to blame their God Yahweh, who was supposed to defend them. Yet Israel did not blame God, but chose to look at themselves instead. When they did that, they realized they had **sinned** greatly against God, becoming thereby the architects of their own destruction. God was **righteous in all** His **deeds, and true in all** His **works** (Dan. 3:27). They had no one to blame but themselves for their plight. That was why their God had given them into **the hands of lawless enemies** and to **an unjust king, the most wicked in the world**. Nebuchadnezzar was but part of the righteous judgment of God.

The judgment was severe indeed. Though God had once promised that they would number more than **the stars of heaven** and **the sand on the seashore**, yet because of their sins they had become **fewer than any** other **nation**. After the catastrophe of 587, there was **no prince, no prophet, and no leader**, there was **no burnt offering**, no **sacrifice**, no **oblation**, and no **incense**—in short, **no place to make an offering before** God. The temple was not simply another building, as a large church is today. It was the only place where Israel could offer sacrifice and **find mercy** from the Lord, for divine mercy and aid came only with the offering of sacrifice. With the temple gone, they were cut off from communion with God.

Yet despite this, they still clung to faith in God's love, praying that **with a contrite heart and a humble spirit** they would **be accepted** by God, as if they had offered **burnt offerings of rams and bulls** and **thousands of fatted lambs**. That is, Israel had nothing left to offer God but their broken hearts and their repentance, and they trusted that this would be as acceptable to their God as if the temple were still standing and able to receive thousands of sacrifices. Such was their confidence in the love of God.

The prayer concludes with a concern for God's glory: "Let them [the nations] **know that You alone are the Lord, and glorious over all the earth.**" At the end of it all, it was not their own happiness that was of ultimate concern, but the glory of their God. The prayer transcends any obsession with their own suffering on earth and focuses instead upon the honor of God in heaven.

The Prayer of Azariah is of more than merely historical value. To us in our culture, with its obsession with rights and with the injustices done to us (whether real or imagined), this prayer provides a welcome and needed antidote. The people of Israel could have turned their eyes to the earth and their gaze inward to their own suffering, languishing and marinating in their own self-pity. But they did not. Rather they turned their eyes to heaven and their gaze to God, offering themselves to Him in repentance. The contrition we find throughout this prayer was no example of pathological self-loathing. Rather it was (to quote Fr. Alexander Schmemann[21]) full of bright sadness, for in offering their repentance to God they put their trust in His forgiveness and in their final restoration.

Today we are tempted to fixate on our own sufferings and on the wrongs we have suffered—and this despite living in North America, one of the most affluent and comfortable areas in the world. When we experience harm we quickly blame God, as if He has somehow let us down in allowing suffering to touch us, and our philosophers ponder and pontificate about "the problem of evil." Solomon's ancient words might have been said regarding our culture: "When a man's folly brings his way to ruin, his heart rages against the Lord" (Prov. 19:3).

The Prayer of Azariah offers another way, the way of penitential introspection and hope. As Job said long ago, "Shall we receive good at the hand of God, and shall we not receive evil?" (Job 2:10). For

---

21   In his classic work *Great Lent: Journey to Pascha* (Crestwood, NY: SVS Press, 1974).

sinners like us, repentance is always timely. Daily we ask our Father for our bread and for the forgiveness of our trespasses, and that He would deliver us by His marvelous works. But of even greater concern to us is that His Name be hallowed and His will be done on earth, as it is in heaven. This is our most profound desire and our constant cry—that the nations may know that He alone is the Lord and glorious over all the earth.

The Hymn of the Three Young Men

[46] And the king's servants who threw them in did not cease stoking the furnace with naphtha, pitch, tow, and brush. [47] And the flame shot out above the furnace forty-nine cubits, [48] and it broke through and burned those of the Chaldeans whom it caught near the furnace. [49] But the angel of the Lord came down into the furnace to be with Azariah and his companions, and shook the flame of fire out of the furnace, [50] and made the midst of the furnace like a moist breeze blowing through, so that the fire did not touch them at all or hurt or trouble them.

[51] Then the three, as with one mouth, sang and glorified and blessed God in the furnace, saying:

[52] "Blessed are You, O Lord, God of our fathers,
to be highly praised and highly exalted forever;
And blessed is Your glorious, holy Name
to be highly praised and highly exalted forever.

[53] Blessed are You in the temple of Your holy glory
to be extolled and highly glorified forever.

[54] Blessed are You upon the throne of Your kingdom
to be extolled and highly exalted forever.

[55] Blessed are You, who sit upon cherubim and behold the depths,
to be praised and highly exalted forever.

[56] Blessed are You in the firmament of heaven
to be sung and glorified forever.

57 Bless the Lord, all you works of the Lord,
sing hymns and highly exalt Him forever.
58 Bless the Lord, you heavens,
sing hymns and highly exalt Him forever.
59 Bless the Lord, you angels of the Lord,
sing hymns and highly exalt Him forever.
60 Bless the Lord, all you waters above the heavens,
sing hymns and highly exalt Him forever.
61 Bless the Lord, all you powers,
sing hymns and highly exalt Him forever.
62 Bless the Lord, you sun and moon,
sing hymns and highly exalt Him forever.
63 Bless the Lord, you stars of heaven,
sing hymns and highly exalt Him forever.
64 Bless the Lord, all you rain and dew,
sing hymns and highly exalt Him forever.
65 Bless the Lord, all you winds,
sing hymns and highly exalt Him forever.
66 Bless the Lord, you fire and heat,
sing hymns and highly exalt Him forever.
67 Bless the Lord, you winter cold and summer heat,
sing hymns and highly exalt Him forever.
68 Bless the Lord, you dews and snows,
sing hymns and highly exalt Him forever.
69 Bless the Lord, you nights and days,
sing hymns and highly exalt Him forever.
70 Bless the Lord, you light and darkness,
sing hymns and highly exalt Him forever.
71 Bless the Lord, you ice and cold,
sing hymns and highly exalt Him forever.
72 Bless the Lord, you frosts and snows,
sing hymns and highly exalt Him forever.
73 Bless the Lord, you lightning and clouds,

sing hymns and highly exalt Him forever.

74 Let the earth bless the Lord;
let it sing hymns and highly exalt Him forever.

75 Bless the Lord, you mountains and hills,
sing hymns and highly exalt Him forever.

76 Bless the Lord, all you things growing in the earth,
sing hymns and highly exalt Him forever.

77 Bless the Lord, you springs,
sing hymns and highly exalt Him forever.

78 Bless the Lord, you seas and rivers,
sing hymns and highly exalt Him forever.

79 Bless the Lord, you sea-monsters and all that move in the waters,
sing hymns and highly exalt Him forever.

80 Bless the Lord, all you birds of heaven,
sing hymns and highly exalt Him forever.

81 Bless the Lord, all you beasts and cattle,
sing hymns and highly exalt Him forever.

82 Bless the Lord, O sons of men,
sing hymns and highly exalt Him forever.

83 Bless the Lord, O Israel,
sing hymns and highly exalt Him forever.

84 Bless the Lord, O priests of the Lord,
sing hymns and highly exalt Him forever.

85 Bless the Lord, O servants of the Lord,
sing hymns and highly exalt Him forever.

86 Bless the Lord, O spirits and souls of the righteous,
sing hymns and highly exalt Him forever.

87 Bless the Lord, O holy and humble in heart,
sing hymns and highly exalt Him forever.

88 Bless the Lord, O Hananiah, Azariah, and Mishael,
sing hymns and highly exalt Him forever;
for He has rescued us from Hades and saved us from the hand
of death,

and delivered us from the midst of the burning fiery furnace;
from the midst of the fire He has delivered us.
89 Give thanks to the Lord, for He is good,
for His mercy endures forever.
90 Bless Him, all who worship the Lord, the God of gods,
sing hymns and give Him thanks,
for His mercy endures forever."

After the Prayer of Azariah we find a long liturgical hymn, commonly called "The Hymn of the Three Young Men," sometimes known in the Western liturgical tradition as the *Benedicite* (from the Latin words of the line, "bless, all you works of the Lord"). It was possibly meant for antiphonal singing, repeating as a refrain the words, "sing hymns and highly exalt Him forever" (compare Ps. 136).

The narrator introduces the hymn with a connecting bit of prose, telling how the king's servants continued to feed the fire to such an extent that **the flame shot out above the furnace forty-nine cubits**—about another seventy feet—even to the point of burning **the Chaldeans** standing around it (a detail already related in the original text in v. 22, though there those throwing the Jews into the fiery furnace were not Chaldeans/priestly sages but "mighty men of valor"). The prose continues, **But the angel of the Lord came down into the furnace to be with Azariah and his companions, and shook the flame of fire out of the furnace**, and **the three, as with one mouth, sang, glorified, and blessed God in the furnace, saying**, followed by the long hymn itself. (The mention of the angel of the Lord descending with the youths into the flame spoils the drama of the original tale, where we first learn of the deliverance of the youths through the astonishment of King Nebuchadnezzar.)

Like the Prayer of Azariah, the Hymn of the Three Young Men

interrupts the flow of the narrative, for it contains little to connect it remotely with the circumstances related in the story. Further, it is unlikely that Nebuchadnezzar, having seen the vision of the angel in the fire, would have waited the long time necessary for them to chant the hymn before removing them from the furnace. Like the prayer, the hymn deserves to be considered on its own.

The hymn is a paean of praise. It begins by blessing God in **the temple of** His **glory**—that is, in heaven—proclaiming Him as the serene Sovereign over all the earth. It continues with a joyful recognition that everything that exists, both in heaven and on earth and even in the deep abyss of the sea, finds its unity in the world and its purpose in life in praising God. The hymn goes on at great length as it marches through the earth, calling each creature in turn to **sing hymns and highly exalt** God **forever.**

Everything in the universe—the high **heavens** above and the **angels** and the **waters above the heavens** and the **powers** inhabiting the heavenlies—every single thing is summoned to take its part in the cosmic doxology. The distant **sun and moon**, the **stars**—none are left out. Every force of nature—**winter cold** and **summer heat** and **winds** and **frosts** and **lightning**—each is called forth to give its song. The **rivers**, the **springs**, all the sources of life lift up a cry to the Creator. Even the untamable Leviathan and **sea-monsters** in the fearsome abyss (in some religions, an image of chaos in opposition to the gods) forms part of the cosmic choir. All the **sons of men**, led by **Israel** and its **priests**, find their place here. This is a daring vision, for the hymnographer hereby declares that all of creation finds its unity not just in Israel's God, but also around Israel itself as the leader of the world's praises.

Today we may miss the depth of insight this involved, for we take for granted that God is the Creator of all nature. It was otherwise in the ancient world, where the forces of nature were considered as divine, each with its own independent existence and claiming its own cultic worship. The hymn defiantly and exuberantly declares that these things are not gods at all but unite in the worship of Israel's Lord. The heavens above, and the sun and the moon and the stars of heaven—everything they see when they look up belongs to God. The snow and the winds, the winter cold and the summer heat, lightning and clouds, springs and rivers—everything they see when they look around them also belongs to God. Even the distant and daunting sea-monsters and the fish that move in the unseen depths of the abyss—everything hidden from their sight by the waves of the sea—even they belong to God. Birds, animals, the children of men, and the spirits of souls of the righteous, all alike unite under the single sovereignty of the Lord. Hananiah, Azariah, and Mishael (here given their Hebrew names and referred to in the third person, another sign of the hymn's independent origin) take their places in the vast cosmos, which finds its highest destiny in singing a hymn to God and exalting Him beyond measure unto the ages.

In our own day, when secularism threatens to wipe the cosmos clean of any hint of mystery and transcendence, we need this hymn more than ever. The world is not something to be considered piecemeal and deconstructed, analyzed, marketed, and sold. The world is itself a sacrament and points to God. Every bird in it sings to Him; the thunder crashes for His pleasure; the wind speaks His Name with joy. This hymn bids us open our eyes and see the world as it truly is. People often talk about the magic of childhood, because children take delight in everything around them—infants in their cribs staring in astonishment at their feet, toddlers staring in amazement at flowers and redwoods, older children running with joy into the pounding waves of the seashore. But it is not childhood that is magical but the world. Children just see the world more clearly than anyone else. Their eyes have not yet been blinded, their hearts

not yet weighted down. They can see the world as God made it—
and as the saints see it.

The music of this hymn needs to ring in our heart and drive out
the din that now fills it. We adults walk in a world of concrete and
technology and noise. We reserve our admiration for gadgets and
electronic toys and (worse yet) celebrities, all of which are doomed
to obsolescence and death. Better to look with fresh eyes on things
that live and last, staring with wonder at the mountains and hills,
trembling before the frost and snow, the winter cold and summer
heat, looking up to the sun and the moon and the stars of heaven,
and directing our gaze past them to where they point, to the Creator of all.

It is not accidental that the hymn is arranged in an antiphonal
manner, with a line constantly repeated. A quick and superficial
reading may regard the seemingly endless repetition of the line
sing hymns and highly exalt Him forever as boring, but in fact
this repetition hides its own theological secret. That secret is this:
that praise in its highest form is communal. Like Psalm 136 with
its repeated refrain "for His mercy endures forever," this hymn is
clearly intended to be sung antiphonally, with one person chanting
the varied verses and another group responding with the repeated
refrain. It was never meant to be chanted alone (much less read
alone, as if it were prose). The hymn was composed to be sung in
an assembly.

Nor is this surprising, if we remember that we worshippers on
earth "represent the cherubim," as the Cherubic Hymn of the great
entrance of our Divine Liturgy declares. For the cherubim and the
seraphim do not sing to God individually. Rather they sing to God
antiphonally, as a choir: "*One called to another* and said, 'Holy, holy,
holy is the Lord of hosts; the whole earth is full of His glory'" (Is.
6:3). The Hymn of the Three Young Men not only bids us see the

world as it is and praise God for it. It also bids us remember that we are part of a family of worshippers, a cherubic chorus, and that we find our destiny not only as part of the world, but also as part of the Church of the living God.

DANIEL 4

The King's Madness

God Judges Nebuchadnezzar's Pride and Then Restores Him

IN THE PREVIOUS CHAPTERS, THE NARRATOR FOCUSED UPON King Nebuchadnezzar and reported wonder after wonder, with miracles of increasing magnitude. First Daniel and his three companions experienced God's power in gaining vigor and flesh in a mere ten days; then Daniel received a vision from God to interpret Nebuchadnezzar's dream, thus saving his own life and the lives of all the Chaldeans. Next his three companions experienced an even greater supernatural miracle, which made them immune from the power of fire.

The narrator thus sets up the listener to expect an even greater wonder in the next chapter, and the listener is not disappointed: the mighty Nebuchadnezzar receives yet another dream and its interpretation, fails to heed the divine wonder, and is to all intents and purposes turned into a beast! After the punishment is received in full, God restores the king to his former self, and he then confesses the power of God using the very words of the Jewish Scriptures—a mighty wonder indeed. The story is often called "the madness of King Nebuchadnezzar," but it is more fitly titled "the conversion of King Nebuchadnezzar," since the story revolves around the king learning the lesson of humility and submission to God.

4 ¹ King Nebuchadnezzar, to all peoples, nations, and languages that dwell in all the earth: Your peace be multiplied! ² It seemed good to me to declare the signs and wonders that the Most High God has worked for me.

³ How great are His signs,
and how mighty His wonders!
His kingdom is an everlasting kingdom,
and His dominion is from generation to generation.

⁴ I, Nebuchadnezzar, was at ease in my house and flourishing in my palace. ⁵ I saw a dream which terrified me, and the thoughts on my bed and the visions of my head alarmed me. ⁶ Therefore a decree was made by me to bring in before me all the wise men of Babylon, that they might make known to me the interpretation of the dream. ⁷ Then the astrologers, the enchanters, the Chaldeans, and the soothsayers came in, and I told the dream before them, but they did not make known to me its interpretation. ⁸ But at last Daniel came in before me—he whose name is Belteshazzar, according to the name of my god; in him is a spirit of the holy gods—and I told the dream before him, saying: ⁹ "Belteshazzar, chief of the astrologers, because I know that the spirit of the holy gods is in you, and no secret baffles you, explain to me the visions of my dream that I have seen and its interpretation."

The chapter begins by administering a literary jolt—in all other chapters the narrator spoke in his own voice, referring to the king in the third person, but here, without any prior warning or explanation, we begin with the voice of King Nebuchadnezzar himself. We hear a confession that the king sent out to all his subjects, spoken in the first person singular. How and why are we hearing from this impulsive, murderous pagan king? The literary stage in the previous stories was filled with a multitude of characters, such as astrologers, enchanters, Chaldeans, men of valor, men at the court, Daniel and his three companions. All have now vanished, and the king steps alone onto the bare stage and begins to speak. The abrupt change from Jewish narration to pagan confession seizes the interest of the listener and draws him into the story.

The confession begins like an epistle or a royal decree: **King Nebuchadnezzar, to all peoples, nations and languages that dwell in all the earth: Your peace be multiplied!** The king of all the earth begins with uncharacteristic modesty: **it seemed good to me to declare the signs and wonders that the Most High God has worked for me.** Here we find no typical royal self-aggrandizement, but a humble declaration of God's glory. The listener draws closer to find out what could possibly have happened to the king. His interest is piqued all the more when the king begins to sound like a Jew: **How great are His signs, and how mighty His wonders!**[22] He even quotes the Psalter: **His kingdom is an everlasting kingdom, and his dominion is from generation to generation** (compare Ps. 145:13). Adding to the solemnity of this opening confession, the words of verse 3 are in poetry, not prose.

This international encyclical begins by recounting the king's experience. As if to stress the supernatural element, the king emphasizes that the dream he is about to recount came unbidden. He was not looking for a revelation but was simply **at ease in** his **house and flourishing in** his **palace.** (A hint of the dream to come may perhaps be seen in the verb "flourishing," which is often used of trees "flourishing" or "greening"; compare Ps. 92:14; Hos. 14:8.) Then God once again intervened in the king's life to give a dream: **I saw a dream which terrified me, and the visions of my head alarmed me.**

The similarity to Nebuchadnezzar's previous experience (narrated

---

22 Compare the pairing of signs and wonders in Ex. 7:3; Deut. 6:22; 13:2.

in 2:1) leads the listener to expect a similar outcome—more threats for those unable to disclose the dream, especially when he once again sends out a **decree** to **bring in all the wise men of Babylon** to **make known the interpretation of the dream**. This time, however, there is a difference, for the king readily discloses the content of the dream. But all in vain, for none of **the astrologers, the enchanters, the Chaldeans,** or **the soothsayers** could make known the dream's **interpretation**.

Long lists are important in the Book of Daniel and usually serve a satiric purpose. Here the purpose is to highlight the futility of merely human wisdom—however many are massed together, none can discover the meaning of the dream except Daniel, to whom God has revealed divine wisdom. In the king's first-person narrative, he explains that Daniel came in last of all.[23] The king shares what the listener to the narrative already knows, that Daniel is also named **Belteshazzar** after **the name** of Nebuchadnezzar's **god** and divine lord Bel, and that in him **is the spirit of the holy gods**.[24] He is further commended as **the chief of the astrologers**. Surely he can explain the dream of the king.

> 10 "As to the visions of my head while on my bed: I was
> looking, and behold!—a tree in the midst of the earth, and
> its height was great!
> 11 The tree grew and became strong;
> its height reached to the sky,
> and it could be seen to the end of all the earth.
> 12 Its foliage was lovely,

---

23 Given Daniel's track record, why was he not called first? In the tale, of course, he must be called last to increase the drama of the narrative.

24 Not "the Spirit of the holy God"; compare comments for 3:25. In the world of Nebuchadnezzar, the phrase meant something like "in whom is a supernatural spirit and power."

its fruit abundant,
and in it was food for all.
The beasts of the field found shade under it;
the birds of the sky dwelt in its branches,
and all flesh was fed from it.

¹³ I saw in the visions of my head on my bed, and behold!—a
watcher, a holy one, coming down from heaven!

¹⁴ He cried aloud and said thus: 'Cut down the tree and cut off
its branches.
Strip off its leaves and scatter its fruit.
Let the beasts flee from under it,
and the birds from its branches.

¹⁵ But leave the stump of its roots in the earth,
bound with a fetter of iron and bronze,
in the tender grass of the field.
Let him be wet with the dew of heaven,
and let him share with the beasts
in the grass of the earth.

¹⁶ Let his heart be changed from that of a man;
let him be given the heart of a beast,
and let seven times pass over him.

¹⁷ This sentence is by the decree of the watchers,
and the decision by the word of the holy ones,
that the living may know
that the Most High rules in the kingdom of men,
and He gives it to whomever He will,
and sets over it the lowliest of men.'

¹⁸ This dream I, King Nebuchadnezzar, saw. And you, Belteshazzar, tell its interpretation, because all the wise men of my kingdom are not able to make known to me the interpretation, but you are able, for a spirit of the holy gods is in you."

Trusting in Daniel's professional and supernatural gifts, Nebuchadnezzar relates his dream. He **was looking and behold! a tree in the midst of the earth, and its height was great!** In fact **its height reached to the sky and could be seen to the end of all the earth.** It provided **food for all; the beasts of the field found shade under it,** and **the birds of the sky dwelt in its branches.** Here we find a clear echo of the parable of Ezekiel 31, which described Pharaoh king of Egypt under the figure of a mighty cedar tree. In this tree, "all the birds of the air made their nests in its boughs, under its branches all the beasts of the field brought forth their young, and under its shadow dwelt all great nations" (Ezek. 31:6). Cedars and huge trees were an obvious image of pride (compare Is. 2:12–13: "The Lord of Hosts has a day against all that is proud and lofty; against all the cedars of Lebanon, lofty and lifted up"), and so we are not surprised to find the image of Nebuchadnezzar's prideful glory presented under the image of a great tree. As the tree could be seen to the end of the earth, so his kingdom reached to the earth's end, and all the great nations dwelt under the shade of the Babylonian king.

Then comes a disturbing feature of the dream, the reason the king was **terrified** and **alarmed** (v. 5). For **a watcher, a holy one**, came **down from heaven** and decreed doom for this mighty tree: "**Cut down the tree and cut off its branches.**" The term **watcher**—a holy angel tasked with supervising affairs on earth—is very prominent in the postexilic literature. For example, in the *Book of Enoch*, a composite book dating from the second and first centuries BC, we find a number of references to such Watchers (such as Enoch 1:5; 10:9; 12:4; 13:10; 15:2), and also in the intertestamental *The Testament of Reuben*. It was part of the development of the concept of angels throughout the Old Testament.[25]

---

25 In the early parts of the Old Testament, such as the Law, angels are more

Here the term is used to stress that events on earth find their ultimate cause in heaven. Kings like Nebuchadnezzar may imagine they rule over the earth, but in reality it is God's will that is finally done, and the flow of history is directed by Him to serve His purposes. The decree of the heavenly Watcher is the true cause for what transpires in Babylon.

The decree was a disturbing one: the mighty tree was to be reduced to a mere log, now useless to all the birds and beasts that once dwelt under its shade and depended on the tree for life and security. The imagery of the dream is quite fluid (as dream imagery often is), so it alternates between talking about a tree and a man. The tree was **cut down** to a mere **stump**, but the man is **bound with a fetter of iron and bronze** (for why would one bind a tree?), and he is left to **be wet with the dew of heaven** and to **share with the beasts in the grass of the earth**—grazing among the grasses like an animal. Indeed, **his heart** was to be **changed from that of a man** to that of a **beast**. Worse yet, the affliction was not a passing episode but was to last for **seven times**, or years. It was announced **that this sentence is by the decree of the watchers** and so could not be challenged or changed. The doom was fixed and sure. This was Nebuchadnezzar's dream, and he said that **all the wise men of** his **kingdom** were **not able to make known** its **interpretation**. Surely Belteshazzar could help?

---

or less anonymous messengers who perform God's will, sometimes barely distinguishable from God Himself (Ex. 23:21). They are seen on earth, but are identified with their tasks, so that they do not present themselves to men as individuals. Thus when Manoah and his wife ask the name of the angel who foretold the birth of their son Samson in order to name the child after him, the angel simply replies, "Why do you ask my name, seeing it is wonderful?" and ascends to heaven in a burst of flame (Judg. 13:17f). It is not until after Israel had mixed with the nations in the exile that angels came to the fore as individuals with names and more differentiated tasks (e.g. Zech. 1:7f). Some see in the use of the term evidence of a late date for the story.

[19] Then Daniel, whose name was Belteshazzar, was stunned for a moment, and his thoughts alarmed him. So the king spoke and said, "Belteshazzar, do not let the dream or its interpretation alarm you." Belteshazzar answered and said, "My lord, may the dream be for those who hate you, and its interpretation for your enemies! [20] The tree that you saw, which grew and became strong, whose height reached to the sky and which could be seen throughout all the earth, [21] whose foliage was lovely and its fruit abundant, in which was food for all, under which the beasts of the field dwelt, and in whose branches dwelt the birds of the heaven— [22] it is you, O king, who have grown and become strong, and your greatness has grown and reaches to the sky, and your dominion to the end of the earth. [23] And whereas the king saw a watcher, a holy one, coming down from heaven and saying, 'Cut down the tree and destroy it, but leave its stump of its roots in the earth, bound with a fetter of iron and bronze in the tender grass of the field; let him be wet with the dew of heaven, and let him share with the beasts of the field, till seven times pass over him.' [24] This is the interpretation, O king, and this is the sentence of the Most High, which has come upon my lord the king: [25] you shall be driven from men; your dwelling shall be with the beasts of the field, and you shall be fed grass like oxen. You shall be wet with the dew of heaven, and seven times shall pass over you, till you know that the Most High rules the kingdom of men and gives it to whomever He wills. [26] And as it was commanded to leave the stump of the roots of the tree, your kingdom shall be assured to you, after you have realized that Heaven rules. [27] Therefore, O king, let my counsel be acceptable to you: break off your sins by practicing righteousness and your iniquities by showing mercy to the poor. Perhaps there may be a lengthening of your prosperity."

Daniel immediately understood the dream, and so horrific was the sentence that he was **stunned for a moment** and unable to speak. Nebuchadnezzar could see Daniel's distress and encouraged him to relate the dream's meaning nonetheless. This rather tender and human exchange serves to underscore the horrific severity of the sentence (for Daniel had to be coaxed to share it) and also serves to secure some of our sympathy for the king so that we are cheered by his repentance and restoration.

In response to the king's encouragement,[26] Daniel, as a loyal subject, cries from the heart, "**My lord, may the dream be for those who hate you, and its interpretation for your enemies!**" (Daniel's sympathy for his sovereign again serves to reinforce our sympathy for him.) He then goes on to relate what the dream reveals—that by the judgment of **the Most High**, mighty Nebuchadnezzar has been sentenced to be **driven from men,** so that his **dwelling shall be with the beasts of the field**, and he will **be fed grass like oxen**, living outside like an animal, **wet with the dew of heaven**. His mind will undergo a severe breakdown, so that he will regard himself as an animal and live like one. This will last for seven long years, until he acknowledges that **the Most High rules the kingdom of men**. God gives royal sovereignty to whom He will, so that Nebuchadnezzar's power comes not from his own merit or might but simply as God's gift.

Daniel hastens to relate the hopeful detail at the end of the dream: though the tree was chopped down and stripped of all its foliage and branches, yet **the stump of the roots** remained. That means that recovery is possible—after, of course, he has learned the lesson and **realized that Heaven** (i.e., God) **rules**.[27]

---

26   Narrated in v. 19 in the third person (i.e., "the king said," not "I Nebuchadnezzar said"). Such a slipping into the third person suggests that the entire story is a third-person narration, rather than an historical encyclical of Nebuchadnezzar. See also the third-person narration in vv. 28–33.

27   The substitution of "heaven" for "God" was characteristic of late postexilic

Daniel, though not asked for his advice or **counsel**, out of compassion for his king adds an exhortation to repentance, one common to the prophetic tradition. Perhaps the dread sentence can be avoided if Nebuchadnezzar repents. After all, the sentence of imminent death for King Hezekiah, delivered by the prophet Isaiah, was changed after the king repented (Is. 38:1–5). Maybe King Nebuchadnezzar can find a similar reprieve and **a lengthening of** his **prosperity** if he too repents. Accordingly, Daniel advises him to **break off** his **sins by practicing righteousness** and by **showing mercy to the poor**. If he does this, perhaps God will relent.

It was a bold thing to say to such a king (or to any powerful person). Powerful rich men in antiquity gave little thought to what we might call social reforms, but that is just what Daniel counseled. The word **righteousness** in postexilic Judaism came to mean not just righteousness in general but almsgiving in particular, and so it is no surprise that the Septuagint translates the word as "almsgiving." The duty of almsgiving was much stressed by the postexilic Old Testament: Tobit mentions it three times (4:7; 12:9; 14:11), and Sirach 17:22 mentions it as a signet right with the Lord (i.e., precious to Him). In the Hellenistic period, the word *righteousness* primarily referred to almsgiving. That such a meaning is foremost here is apparent from its pairing with **showing mercy to the poor**.[28]

> [28] All this came upon King Nebuchadnezzar. [29] At the end of the twelve months he was walking in the royal palace of Babylon, [30] and the king answered and said, "Is not this Babylon the great, which I have built for a royal dwelling by my mighty power and for the glory of my majesty?" [31] While the word was still in the king's mouth, there fell a voice from heaven:

Judaism; it is used nowhere else in the Old Testament.

28   Another evidence of a late date.

"King Nebuchadnezzar, to you it is spoken: the kingdom has departed from you! [32] And you shall be driven from among men, and your dwelling shall be with the beasts of the field, and you shall be fed grass like oxen; and seven times shall pass over you, until you know that the Most High rules the kingdom of men, and He gives it to whomever He wills." [33] That very moment the word was fulfilled concerning Nebuchadnezzar; he was driven from men and ate grass like oxen; his body was wet with the dew of heaven till his hair had grown like eagles' feathers and his nails like birds' claws. [34] And at the end of the days, I, Nebuchadnezzar, lifted my eyes to heaven, and my understanding returned to me; and I blessed the Most High and praised and honored Him who lives forever,

for His dominion is an everlasting dominion,
and His kingdom is from generation to generation.
[35] All the dwellers on the earth are accounted as nothing;
He does according to His will in the host of heaven
and among the dwellers on the earth.
No one can stay His hand
or say to Him, "What are You doing?"

[36] At the same time my understanding returned to me, and the glory of my kingdom, my majesty and splendor returned to me. My counselors and lords sought me, I was settled in my kingdom, and still more greatness was added to me. [37] Now I, Nebuchadnezzar, praise and extol and glorify the King of heaven, for all His works are truth, and His ways justice, and those who walk in pride He is able to humble."

Slipping into the third person, the narrator continues the story. By changing from the first person ("I, King Nebuchadnezzar" as in v. 18) the narrator skillfully pulls back the focus to allow us a more dramatic view of the events, for the listener is enabled to see the horrifying change in the king objectively.

After Daniel's counsel of repentance, Nebuchadnezzar is given an entire **twelve months** to comply. It is only after he fails to use such a long period of grace that the promised judgment falls. Significantly, the stroke falls at precisely the moment the king is exalting and congratulating himself. The historical Nebuchadnezzar was well known for enlarging and beautifying Babylon and for boasting about it. Our narrator focuses on these boasts as precisely the cause of divine judgment. Far from heeding the dream's warning that **the Most High rules the kingdom of men and gives it to whomever He wills** and recognizing that Babylon's greatness is actually the gift of God, Nebuchadnezzar foolishly ascribes all the city's greatness to himself—**Babylon the great** was **built for** *his* **own royal dwelling** and **by** *his* **own mighty power, for the glory of** *his* **majesty.**

Such hubris is too much, and the voice of Nebuchadnezzar is immediately answered by the voice of the Most High. A voice from heaven (later known in Hebrew literature as a *bat qol*, the "daughter of a voice," an echo from heaven) announces that the sentence is now to be carried out, and he will be **driven from among men** to make his **dwelling** with **the beasts of the field**. He was graciously given the chance to learn the lesson without experiencing the threatened judgment, but he refused. Now the only way for him to learn that **the Most High rules the kingdom of men** is through seven long years of judgment. The king exalted himself and thought himself greater than any man. Now he will find himself lesser than any man, a mere animal. He must learn that "man in his pomp cannot abide; he is like the beasts that perish" (Ps. 49:20).

The divine sentence was carried out immediately, at that very moment. The king lost all his faculties and became like a beast. He **ate grass like oxen**, remaining outside so that **his body was wet with the dew of heaven.** Moreover **his hair** grew long **like eagles'**

feathers and **his nails like birds' claws**. In this degraded state he languished for the seven long years.[29]

The story climaxes with a dramatic return to use of the first person: **At the end of the days, I, Nebuchadnezzar, lifted my eyes to heaven, and my understanding returned to me; and I blessed the Most High and praised and honored Him who lives forever.** Here we find the greatest miracle yet in these stories—a pagan king praising God as a Jew would. The vocabulary and language are straight from the Hebrew Scriptures (compare Sir. 18:1 and Is. 40:17), including a verbatim quote again from Psalm 145:13.

The king has indeed learned his lesson. He did not become a Jew (i.e., he did not become circumcised and begin to keep the Sabbath), but he did honor the Most High and acknowledge His complete cosmic sovereignty, both over the host of heaven and among the dwellers on earth. We can find no trace in his words that Nebuchadnezzar acknowledged the sovereignty or indeed even the existence of other gods. Instead, he speaks like a good biblical monotheist.

As a divine reward for such repentance and insight, all his former glory was restored. His majesty and splendor were returned, his counselors and lords sought him out as before, and he was settled and established in his rule. More than this, still more greatness was added to him by God—a completely happy ending. The story ends with a repetition of the good Jewish moral: one should always **extol and glorify the King of heaven,**[30] **for all His works are truth, and His ways justice, and those who walk in pride He is able to humble.**

---

29 Contemporary Babylonian records mention no such illness of Nebuchadnezzar nor any such break in his long rule. Nor is it likely that he would be allowed to remain as ruler for long in such a state.

30 The title for God "the King of heaven" is found only here in the Old Testament, though it is found in the intertestamental 1 Esdras 4:46—another indication of a late date.

THE STORY OF THE FALL AND RESTORATION OF KING Nebuchadnezzar is the most amazing of all these amazing stories yet considered. The narrator of the Book of Daniel continues to take his listener for a roller-coaster ride of wonders—Nebuchadnezzar, fearsome villain of the last two stories, issues an international epistle praising the Most High God. We learn of yet another dream, one which again demonstrates the power of Daniel and his God over the useless Chaldeans. Then the king loses his mind and is forced to live like an animal, grazing freely with the beasts, degenerating into a wretched state with long nails and uncut hair! One does not ask why such a wonder left no trace in any history or why the Babylonian rulers would have allowed it to continue for so long—the story catches one up and carries its listeners along with no chance to question until its final resolution. A Jew would take immense satisfaction in the fate of the king—the proud conqueror of Judea, the one who carried away their king and the holy vessels of the temple (1:2) forced to eat grass like the oxen and be exposed to the elements like an animal. And the resolution would be more satisfying still, for at the end the king effectively converts to monotheism, praising the King of heaven.

Even apart from the emotional satisfaction derived from the story by those in postexilic Israel, the tale also teaches important truths: all accomplishments, gifts, and power come solely as gifts from God, and all that occurs on the world stage ultimately fulfills His will. Not, of course, that God causes people to act as they do so that free will is eliminated, but rather that all human choices, decisions, and actions come together to serve His ultimate design. God rules the kingdom of men, whatever the men themselves may imagine. If we sometimes feel the world is spinning out of control, let us remember the words of the watchers. God sets over the kingdoms of the world whomever He chooses.

We find another truth here as well and learn that self-exaltation provokes the judgment of God. We do not need to be king of Babylon to exalt ourselves, for the tendency to attribute our successes to our own talents and hard work is a universal one and a timeless temptation. We may not be struck down with such a psychosis as was Nebuchadnezzar, but exalting ourselves, heedless of humility, always comes at a price. Even before the watcher pronounced sentence, we knew that pride goes before destruction and a haughty spirit before a fall (Prov. 16:18).

With Nebuchadnezzar's final doxology of praise to the Most High, and his kingship restored and enlarged by God, the Book of Daniel leaves him for good. The next story looks at the Babylonian court in its final hours and narrates a tale even more amazing than any of the others. The ride continues.

DANIEL 5

The Writing on the Wall

God Responds to Belshazzar's Blasphemy with a Judgment of Doom

5 ¹ Belshazzar the king made a great feast for a thousand of his lords and drank wine in front of the thousand. ² When he tasted the wine, Belshazzar commanded to bring the gold and silver vessels which his father Nebuchadnezzar had taken from the temple which was in Jerusalem, that the king and his lords, his wives, and his concubines might drink from them. ³ Then they brought the gold vessels that had been taken from the temple of the House of God which was in Jerusalem; and the king and his lords, his wives, and his concubines drank from them. ⁴ They drank wine and praised the gods of gold and silver, bronze and iron, wood, and stone. ⁵ At that moment the fingers of a man's hand appeared and wrote on the plaster of the wall of the king's palace opposite the lampstand; and the king saw the palm of the hand that wrote. ⁶ Then the king's color changed, and his thoughts alarmed him, so that the knots of his loins were loosened and his knees knocked against each other. ⁷ The king cried aloud to bring in the enchanters, the Chaldeans, and the soothsayers. The king answered and said to the wise men of Babylon, "Whoever reads this writing, and declares to me its interpretation, shall be clothed with purple and have a chain of gold about his neck; and he shall be the

third ruler in the kingdom." [8] Now all the king's wise men came,
but they were not able to read the writing, or make known to
the king the interpretation. [9] Then King Belshazzar was greatly
alarmed, his color was changed, and his lords were perplexed.

The scene opens with a **great feast** of a **thousand** people, hosted by
Belshazzar the king, whose **father** was **Nebuchadnezzar**.[31] (This
relationship is stressed repeatedly throughout the narrative.) After
he had **tasted the wine** (meaning possibly after he was drunk),
he issued a command that was outrageous even in ancient times:
**the gold and silver vessels which his father Nebuchadnezzar
had taken from the temple which was in Jerusalem** should be
brought in that **the king, his lords, his wives, and his concubines might drink from them**. Even pagans understood that the
cultic vessels of a religion ought never to be used as mere drinking
vessels at a drunken debauch. (In Is. 52:11, exilic Israel is bidden
to "purify yourselves" before touching the sacred vessels and carrying them home.) The act was spectacularly sacrilegious even by
pagan standards. The narrator stresses that the sacred vessels were
not only to be handled and drunk from by the king, but even by his
concubines. The concubines' presence here serves to emphasize the
scandalous vulgarity of the king and increase the outrage of using
the temple vessels as common drinking cups.

---

31 History records two problems here: Belshazzar was not the son of
    Nebuchadnezzar, but the son of Nebuchadnezzar's successor and Babylon's
    last king, Nabonidus, and there is no record of any biological connection
    with Nebuchadnezzar. Also, Belshazzar was not king at the fall of Babylon,
    but only the coregent, ruling in Babylon for his father, who was in Arabia.
    As such, Belshazzar could not perform the royal function of presiding at
    the Babylonian New Year festival. Though the term "king" could be used
    here only loosely, the emphasis of the continuity between "father" and "son"
    indicates that the narrator intends us to see Belshazzar as king in exactly the
    same way as Nebuchadnezzar was.

Worse yet, the pagans not only drank from them but also **praised the gods of gold and silver, bronze, iron, wood, and stone** (the narrator details the long list of materials used to stress the multiplicity and stupidity of idolatry). Given the pairing of "drinking" with "praising," this latter probably refers to pouring out a libation to those gods from the sacred vessels—the ultimate blasphemy, using Yahweh's holy things in the service of idols.

The use of the holy vessels taken from the temple ties this story with the introductory story in chapter one (see 1:2), linking the Jews' deportation to Babylon with Babylon's final fall—and perhaps even hinting that it was this blasphemy against the Jewish God that caused that final fall. The sacrilegious use of the temple furnishings would have particular resonance for those in Maccabean times who saw their temple put to such sacrilegious use by Antiochus Epiphanes.

The blasphemy was immediately answered. At that very moment, the **fingers of a man's hand appeared and wrote on the plaster of the wall** behind the king's head. The picture is a freakish and eerie one, with a large hand, disconnected from everything, writing an inscription on the wall. Kings would often inscribe an account of their military triumphs in public where all could see them and reflect on the power of the king. Here was the public inscription of the Jewish God the king has just provoked. The narrator mentions that a **lampstand** was nearby, so that the writing could be easily seen.

With his usual consummate skill, the narrator does not immediately describe what the hand wrote, only the reaction of the king: his **color changed**, as all the blood drained from his face, and **the knots of his loins were loosened and his knees knocked against each other**. The narrator paints us a comic picture, portraying the king for the vulgar and cowardly buffoon he was. At the beginning of the feast he was the daring potentate, unafraid of provoking the Jewish God by his act of sacrilege. Now he is a quivering puddle of terror. It is possible that the phrase **the knots of his loins were loosened** indicates that he lost control of his bowels and soiled himself—a comic picture indeed. We see the same contrast between drunken high spirits and cowering anxiety sweep the whole room, as the raucous and bawdy banquet suddenly turns quiet, and the blasphemous banqueters stare in fear at the terrible words and wonder what doom they portend.

Predictably (after reading of Nebuchadnezzar's repeated calls for help from his wise men), Belshazzar also cries aloud for **the enchanters, the Chaldeans, and the soothsayers**. The constantly repeated long list of professional sages has now become a kind of running joke in the Book of Daniel: the king always calls for the same huge crowd of sages, and they always prove themselves completely useless. Their presence serves only to demonstrate the superiority of Daniel and that of his God. The king offers the usual incentives in his pompous decree: **whoever reads this writing and declares its interpretation** shall be **clothed with purple** (the royal color, indicating great honor), and **have a chain of gold about his neck**, and **be third ruler in the kingdom**.

There is some doubt regarding to what this last gift refers. Some suggest the term hearkens back to an Akkadian title in Babylon, indicating a *triumvir*, a high government official. The details hardly matter, for the narrator only mentions these passing vanities and worthless rewards so that Daniel can refuse them. Despite these incentives, after **all the wise men came**, they were **not able to read the writing**. It is another gratifying spectacle: all the wisdom, lore, education, and brilliance of Babylon assembles, and they can make neither head nor tail of the matter. So much for Babylon. Since the words were supernaturally given and a doom feared, their failure is further cause for fear. Once again the color drains from the king's face, and his lords also are nonplussed.

> [10] The queen, because of the words of the king and his lords, came into the banqueting hall. The queen answered and said, "O king, live forever! Do not let your thoughts alarm you, nor let your color change. [11] There is a man in your kingdom in whom is a spirit of the holy gods. And in the days of your father, light and insight and wisdom, like the wisdom of the gods, were found in him; and King Nebuchadnezzar your father—your father the king—made him chief of the astrologers, enchanters, Chaldeans, and soothsayers. [12] Because a remarkable spirit, knowledge, understanding to interpret dreams, explaining puzzles, and resolving knots were found in this Daniel, whom the king named Belteshazzar, now let Daniel be called, and he will declare the interpretation." [13] Then Daniel was brought in before the king. The king spoke and said to Daniel, "Are you that Daniel who is one of the exiles of Judah, whom my father the king brought from Judah? [14] I have heard of you, that a spirit of the gods is in you, and that light and understanding and remarkable wisdom are found in you. [15] Now the wise men, the enchanters, have been brought in before me that they should read this writing and make known to me its interpretation, but they were not able to declare the interpretation of the thing. [16] And I have heard of you that you can give interpretations and explain problems. Now if you can read the writing and declare to me its interpretation, you shall be clothed with purple and have a chain of gold about your neck and shall be the third ruler in the kingdom." [17] Then Daniel answered and said before the king, "Let your gifts be for yourself, and give your presents to another; nevertheless I will read the writing to the king and declare to him the interpretation. [18] As for you, O king, the Most High God gave a kingdom

and greatness, splendor, and majesty to Nebuchadnezzar your father. [19] And because of the greatness that He gave him, all peoples, nations, and languages shook and feared before him. Whomever he wished, he executed; whomever he wished, he kept alive; whomever he wished, he exalted; and whomever he wished, he humbled. [20] But when his heart was lifted up, and his spirit was hardened to rebel, he was deposed from the throne of his kingdom, and his splendor was taken from him. [21] Then he was driven from the sons of men, his heart was made like the beasts, and his dwelling was with the wild donkeys. They fed him grass like oxen, and his body was wet with the dew of heaven, till he knew that the Most High God rules the kingdom of men and appoints over it whomever He wills. [22] But as for you, his son, Belshazzar, you have not humbled your heart, even though you knew all this, [23] but you have lifted yourself up against the Lord of heaven. They have brought before you the vessels of His House, and you and your lords, your wives and your concubines, have drunk wine from them. And you have praised the gods of silver and gold, bronze and iron, wood and stone, which do not see or hear or know; and the God in whose hand is your breath and whose are all your ways, you have not glorified. [24] Then the palm of the hand was sent from Him, and this writing was inscribed."

Then, though not summoned, at just the right moment, **the queen came into the banqueting hall**. It is apparent that she is the queen mother, not the wife of Belshazzar (his wives are already there; v. 2). Given that Belshazzar is consistently and emphatically portrayed throughout as Nebuchadnezzar's son, this woman therefore must have been Nebuchadnezzar's wife, and as such she was in a position to know all about the experiences of Nebuchadnezzar. The narrator presents her as a woman of sagacity and sense, in stunning contrast to her pathetic and ineffectual son.

She knows that there is **a man in the kingdom in whom is a spirit of the holy gods**, and such is his **light, insight, and wisdom** that **Nebuchadnezzar your father** (she stresses his royal authority again—**your father the king**) made him **chief of the astrologers, enchanters, Chaldeans, and soothsayers**. (Again with the long list!) If the king will call **this Daniel, whom the king named Belteshazzar**, the mystery will be solved. Reference to the king naming Daniel Belteshazzar is not an unnecessary detail but serves to remind the listener of all the rest of Daniel's exploits detailed in the stories.

Belshazzar addresses Daniel as **one of the exiles of Judah**, one gifted with **a spirit of the gods, light, understanding, and remarkable wisdom**. He repeats his dilemma and the offer of reward, and seems completely oblivious of the fact that as one of the Judean exiles, Daniel of all people would surely take great offense at the blasphemous use to which the vessels from the temple were being put. Belshazzar seems to think Daniel will only be motivated by hope of getting these rewards and will overlook the sacrilege before his face. The narrator is keen to stress such cluelessness and insensitivity. If Nebuchadnezzar was presented in a positive light in the previous chapter, his "son" is presented in a wholly negative one, richly deserving the death that awaits him.

Not surprisingly, Daniel is abrupt in his reply. Unlike the queen, he does not preface his address with the customary, "O king, live forever!" but simply declines the offer, saying, "**Let your gifts be for yourself**"—in that context and culture, a reply that lacks all courtesy. He then boldly rebukes the king for his insolence, citing the example of **Nebuchadnezzar your father**. The **Most High God gave** him **greatness, splendor, and majesty**, so that his sovereignty was complete and unchallenged. He did whatever he chose. Yet despite these gifts, **when his heart was lifted up, and his spirit**

hardened to rebel, that same God **deposed** him **from the throne** and took all that **splendor** from him. He was **driven from the sons of men**, and **his dwelling was with the wild donkeys**—that is, in the wilderness.

With such an example immediately before him, why did Belshazzar not learn from it? In fact he too **lifted** himself **up against the Lord of heaven** by committing sacrilege with **the vessels of His House**. Daniel is immensely daring in his public rebuke of the king and plainly identifies the Most High God who gave Nebuchadnezzar his kingdom with the God of the Judeans. He also is unsparing in his rebuke of the king's gods, whom he denounces as **gods of silver and gold, bronze and iron, wood and stone, which do not see or hear or know**. It is because the king refused to **glorify** the God of Israel, the Lord of heaven who owns **all** the **ways** of Belshazzar and all the kings of the earth, that **the palm of the hand was sent** from God to inscribe this doom above his head.

In any other circumstance, such a public denunciation of the king and his gods would bring instant and severe retaliation, but Daniel speaks from a heart filled with moral indignation and outrage over the sacrilege standing before his face.

Daniel then proceeds to loosen the knot and resolve the puzzle of the words and their meaning.

> [25] "And this is the writing that was inscribed: MENE, MENE, TEKEL, UPARSIN. [26] This is the interpretation of the thing. MENE: God has numbered your kingdom, and finished it; [27] TEKEL: you have been weighed in the scales and found wanting; [28] PERES: your kingdom is divided and given to the Medes and Persians." [29] Then Belshazzar spoke, and they clothed Daniel with purple and put a chain of gold about his neck, and proclaimed concerning him that he should be the third ruler in the kingdom. [30] In that night Belshazzar, king of

the Chaldeans, was killed, [31] and Darius the Mede received the kingdom, being about sixty-two years old.

Daniel first reads the writing as four words, **MENE, MENE, TEKEL, UPARSIN**. He then continues to interpret those four words, speaking tersely, with no polite courtly rhetoric and no apology for the doom the words contain. The king wants the interpretation? Here it is.

The four words contain puns and wordplays based on monetary weights. It is like saying, "a ton, a ton, a pound, and parts." MENE refers to a weight called a *mina*, but also to the verb meaning "to number." TEKEL refers to another weight, a *shekel*, but also to the verb meaning "to weigh." UPARSIN (the dual plural of *peres*; the *u* means "and") refers to the verb for "to divide" or "to halve." Daniel interprets the monetary weights as an historical prophecy of judgment: the **MENE** means **God** has **numbered** the Babylonian kingdom and **finished it** (as in "its days are numbered"; the doubling of the word *mene* may refer to the finality of the divine decree numbering its days). The **TEKEL** means it has been **weighed in the scales** of divine justice and **found** light and **wanting**. The **PERES** of the final UPARSIN is from the verb meaning "to divide," and it has a double meaning. The Babylonian kingdom has been **divided** and broken up and will pass to **the Medes and Persians**. Of these two, the Persians were the more prominent, as witnessed by the verbal similarity of the word *peres* to the word *Paras* (Persia).

The story ends with Belshazzar bestowing on Daniel the honors he has just refused, a sign of the ridiculous pomp and self-importance of the doomed kingdom. For what can such honors in Babylon mean when Babylon itself is falling to the Medes and the Persians? Belshazzar's meaningless promotion of Daniel serves to stress the futility of Belshazzar's reign and his blindness to what Daniel has just revealed.

In the final sentence, the narrator says in **that** very **night** Babylon fell to its enemies, **Belshazzar was killed,**[32] and **Darius the Mede received the kingdom,**[33] and that the Median conqueror of Babylon was **sixty-two years old** at that time. Thus Belshazzar, in all his absurd pomp, received the just reward for his blasphemy, and with him the entire kingdom of Babylon perished and met its end.

Of all the adventures of Daniel and his companions in Babylon, this is perhaps the most astounding. Belshazzar, drunk at a feast at the time when his city is (we learn afterward) under siege from attackers, stages a daring act of sacrilegious bravado. It is instantly answered by the God whom he has blasphemed, and a disembodied hand is seen writing four words on the wall above his head, evidently the divine response to his blasphemy. As usual, the Chaldeans prove themselves useless, and Daniel is called to save the day. He curtly refuses the proffered rewards, boldly rebukes the king for not honoring his Jewish God, and then translates the meaning of the mysterious words of doom. Soon after that, the city falls and the king is killed (presumably by those storming the city). With these

32 Contemporary Babylonian records say nothing about the death of Belshazzar when Babylon fell, but instead record the capture and exile of its actual final king, Nabonidus, after Cyrus took the city unopposed. As the coregent and son of the king, some suggest that it is likely Belshazzar was not in the city when Cyrus took it, but commanding the Babylonian forces fighting the Persians at Opis.

33 Historical records of that time know of no such ruler as Darius the Mede. The successor to the last Babylonian king, Nabonidus, was Cyrus the Persian, who was indeed about sixty-two years old when he took Babylon without a fight in 538 BC. His reign was followed by that of his son, Cambyses, and then by that of Darius I, who took Babylon after a revolt in 520 BC. It appears the author here conflated the two events of 538 and 520, making Darius the one who took Babylon after the reign of Nabonidus. It is thought he is here styled "the Mede" because of the tradition that Babylon would fall to the Medes (in Is. 13:17f; 21:2–10; Jer. 51:28f).

supernatural and eerie events, the curtain comes down on Babylon and the dynasty of Nebuchadnezzar.

The story is immensely satisfying to any who have suffered oppression and who long for God to rebuke the oppressor and vindicate the truth. If only the proud, apparently invincible ones who grind the faces of the poor with impunity could be so answered by God! If only they could for once see the handwriting on the wall and know of their future doom! If only they could be made to shake with fear before their deserved end as Belshazzar did before his! In this age, God does indeed inscribe doom for the impenitent oppressor, but the reading of the sentence must wait until one steps from this world into the next. The story of Belshazzar reveals that such an inscription of doom has indeed been written against the earth's proud oppressors, even if its writing is invisible to them.

DANIEL 6

Daniel in the Den

God Protects Daniel from the Lions as a Reward for His Integrity

6 [1] It pleased Darius to set over the kingdom one hundred and twenty satraps, to be throughout the whole kingdom; [2] and over these three presidents, of whom Daniel was one, to whom these satraps should give account, so that the king might suffer no injury. [3] Then this Daniel distinguished himself above the presidents and satraps, because a remarkable spirit was in him; and the king planned to appoint him over all the kingdom. [4] So the presidents and satraps sought to find some pretext against Daniel concerning the kingdom; but they were not able to find a pretext or fault, because he was faithful; nor was there any error or fault found in him. [5] Then these men said, "We shall not find any pretext against this Daniel unless we find it against him concerning the law of his god." [6] So these presidents and satraps thronged the king and said thus to him: "King Darius, live forever! [7] All the presidents of the kingdom, the prefects and satraps, the counselors and governors, have consulted together that the king should establish a statute and enforce a ban, that whoever petitions any god or man for thirty days, except you, O king, shall be cast into the pit of lions. [8] Now, O king, establish the ban and sign the document, so that it cannot be changed,

according to the law of the Medes and Persians, which cannot be revoked." [9] Therefore, King Darius signed the document and the ban.

The next story is set in the reign of King Darius. He is described as a great organizer, for **he set over the kingdom one hundred and twenty satraps and over these three presidents, of whom Daniel was one, to whom these satraps should give account**.[34] We see here how the king entrusts Daniel with such a high and important post, making sure that he **might suffer no injury**, possibly through rebellion or graft in the provinces—a sign of his closeness to Daniel and his confidence in him. Daniel further **distinguished himself above** the other two **presidents** and the **satraps**, so that **the king planned to appoint him over all the kingdom** as second in command, under himself.

This plan excited the envy and jealousy of the other presidents and satraps, who doubtless despised Daniel as a foreigner, **one of the exiles from Judah** (v. 13). Accordingly they plotted his fall from the king's grace, but such was Daniel's integrity that they realized the only **pretext** they might find against him was **concerning the law of his god**. They therefore concocted a plan. Those in on the plot were **the presidents and satraps** (v. 4)—possibly not all one hundred and twenty satraps, for most of these were scattered throughout the whole kingdom (v. 1), but at least some of those who were local and close at hand.

Their first move was to **throng the king**—a verb probably indicating they came in a large group to overwhelm the king

---

34 The narrator here conflates "Darius the Mede" with Darius I, who organized the Persian empire into twenty satrapies (not one hundred and twenty). There is no record of the existence of three presidents to whom the satraps were responsible. Perhaps the narrator was thinking of the ostensible Babylonian office of *triumvir* mentioned in 5:7.

emotionally and so coerce him into establishing a law without sufficient forethought. Their prepared story was that all **the presidents, the prefects and satraps, the counselors and governors have consulted together** and reached an impressive and universal consensus—namely that **the king should establish a statute and enforce a ban, that whoever petitions any god or man for thirty days, except** the **king, shall be cast into the pit of lions**. The point of declaring it a **statute** is that as a royal **law of the Medes and Persians** it **cannot be changed** or revoked.[35] Without further thought, the king hearkens to what they present as a popular decree, one calculated to increase the king's glory, and he **signed the document and the ban**.

The picture of a crowd of underlings strong-arming the king does not make the king look very impressive or royal. This is part of the narrator's ongoing satire and invective directed at pagan rulers. If Nebuchadnezzar was painted as an impulsive, proud, and murderous tyrant, and if Belshazzar was painted as a drunken, blasphemous coward, Darius is portrayed as foolish, gullible, and ineffectual. Such are the mighty pagan powers who do not worship the true God.

The proposed law making it a capital offense to offer prayer to any god or petition to any man (presumably the priests) is an extraordinary one, not only because it contains such a harsh penalty for noncompliance (like the decision of 2:5 and the law of 3:4–6), but also because it violates everything known about religion in the ancient world and about Persian religious tolerance in particular. The world of that day was full of gods, and no ruler would dream of outlawing

---

35 There is no trace of such a legal custom in antiquity, apart from here in the Book of Daniel and in the Book of Esther. Presumably kings could change laws and decrees if they chose—as we see for example in Ezra 4:21, where a decree is made with the understanding that it can be overturned in the future. But such a feature is essential to the story.

religious practice, especially for a month. The law is absurd, point-less, and largely incapable of enforcement. One cannot imagine any ruler establishing such a law, but the story requires such a law to be decreed if the plot against Daniel is to be carried out.

> [10] Now when Daniel knew that the document was signed, he went to his house. And in his roof chamber, windows were open to him toward Jerusalem. And three times in the day he knelt on his knees and prayed and gave thanks before his God, as he had done previously. [11] Then those men assembled and found Daniel praying and supplicating before his God. [12] And they came near to the king and spoke concerning the royal ban: "Have you not signed a ban that any man who petitions any god or man within thirty days, except you, O king, shall be cast into the pit of lions?" The king answered and said, "The thing is true, according to the law of the Medes and Persians, which cannot be revoked." [13] So they answered and said before the king, "That Daniel, who is one of the exiles from Judah, does not pay attention to you, O king, or to the ban that you have signed, but makes his petition three times a day." [14] And the king, when he heard these words, was greatly displeased with himself, and set his heart on Daniel to deliver him; and he labored till the going down of the sun to deliver him. [15] Then those men assembled before the king and said to the king, "Know, O king, that it is the law of the Medes and Persians that no ban or statute which the king establishes can be changed." [16] So the king commanded, and they brought Daniel and cast him into the pit of lions. But the king spoke, saying to Daniel, "May your God, whom you serve constantly, deliver you!" [17] Then a stone was brought and laid on the mouth of the pit, [36] and the king sealed it with his own signet and with the

---

36 There is no record in antiquity of lions being kept in pits in the Near East. Indeed, it is difficult to imagine the layout of the pit that could be sealed

signets of his lords, that the purpose concerning Daniel might not be changed.

When **Daniel knew that the document was signed**, he immediately discerned its true intent. But rather than protesting to the king, he simply **went to his house** and continued with his accustomed daily devotion to his God. Once again the serenity and confident composure of Daniel shine through, in contrast to the panic of those around him (compare 2:14). As the prophet Isaiah said, "He who believes will not be in haste" (Is. 28:16, ESV). At his house Daniel had a **roof chamber**, an apartment on the flat roof of his house, with **windows open toward Jerusalem**. It was his pious custom **three times in the day** to pray **on his knees** toward the former site of the temple.

Prayer while kneeling was somewhat unusual; the regular posture for prayer was standing with upraised hands. Prayer while kneeling or prostrate indicated great fervency or distress (compare our Lord's posture in Gethsemane; Luke 22:41). Nor was praying three times a day yet mandated for Jews. That would come later. Nor was there any suggestion that prayer had to be made facing Jerusalem. Solomon had assumed at the dedication of the temple that Israelites throughout the world would pray in that way (1 Kin. 8:29–30, 46–51), but he was referring to prayer *toward the temple*,[37] assuming it would still be standing, not prayer toward a city in which the temple had been destroyed.

In all these things—his posture, the number of times he prayed, and his orientation to Jerusalem—Daniel showed an unusual and

---

by laying a stone over its mouth. But the difficult logistics of the lions' den are no more historically important than the layout and logistics of the fiery furnace in 3:22–23. What matters is their importance to the story.

37 See especially 1 Kin. 8:48: "if they repent and pray to You toward the land, the city, *and the House which I have built.*"

outstanding piety. This had been his custom, hardened into habit by a lifetime of faithfulness to God, and he saw no reason to alter it. Given the choice between the law of the Medes and Persians and the law of his God (vv. 5, 8), he knew which of the two he must choose.

Because Daniel prayed at an open window in his roof chamber, it was not difficult for his envious adversaries to find him **praying and supplicating before his God** as they knew he regularly did. Armed with this damning proof of Daniel's arrogant heedlessness of the king's law (as they would portray it), **they came near to the king** to set the final part of the trap. They asked him to confirm that he did indeed **sign a ban** prohibiting any **petitions** to **any god or man** for **thirty days** and that violators when caught would be **cast into the pit of lions**. He confirmed the obvious, including especially the penalty, obligingly adding that the decree had been made **according to the law of the Medes and Persians, which cannot be revoked**. Exactly. Having these words straight from the king's own mouth, they then spring the trap: they can now loyally report to the king that **Daniel**, one of the suspiciously foreign **exiles from Judah, does not pay attention to you, or to the ban that you signed**. He did not just make a petition to his god once, but three times each day! There was now nothing for it: the law was irrevocable, and Daniel had broken the law and must be cast into the lions' den.

The king was then **greatly displeased with himself**—in other words, he realized he had been played. He **labored till the going down of the sun** to find a way out, possibly consulting his lawyers, sages, and other experts, but all for naught. Daniel's adversaries **assembled before the king** to gang up and bully him once again, reminding him and bidding him **know that it is the law of the Medes and Persians that no ban which the king establishes can**

be changed. The king makes a pathetic picture of absurd helplessness before his subjects. They have thoroughly outwitted him and
refuse to let him have his way. There is nothing the king can do. He
could organize the empire into one hundred and twenty satrapies,
but he cannot save the man he appointed over them.

A final bit of pathos comes with the juxtaposition of Daniel
being **cast into the pit of lions** at the command of the king with
the king's final word to him, "**May your God, whom you serve
constantly, deliver you!**" The Aramaic grammar here presents this
not as a jussive but a declaration—"your God *will* deliver you," but
given the king's agitation, he was not expressing confidence in Daniel's deliverance (as his behavior that night would show). Rather,
the words to Daniel were his sad attempt to comfort his trusted
friend. It was more of a wistful wish than a confession of faith. As if
to make the situation even more hopeless, the narrator adds that a
stone was brought and laid on the mouth of the pit, which **the king
sealed with his own signet and with the signets of his lords** so
that none might tamper with the stone and release Daniel. The seal
did not ensure that the stone would not be moved, only that any
removal would be apparent: at a glance one could see in the morning that Daniel had been there in the pit all night. That the king
himself participated in this only adds to the spectacle of his pathetic
helplessness.

> [18] Then the king went to his palace and spent the night fasting;
> and no diversions were brought before him, and his sleep fled
> him. [19] Then the king arose in the dawn of the day and went
> in haste to the pit of lions. [20] And when he came to the pit, he
> cried out with a grieving voice to Daniel. The king answered
> and said to Daniel, "Daniel, servant of the living God, has your
> God, whom you serve constantly, been able to deliver you
> from the lions?" [21] Then Daniel said to the king, "O king, live

forever! ²² My God sent His angel and shut the mouths of the lions, and they have not harmed me, because innocence was found in me before Him; and also before you, O king, I have done no harm." ²³ Now the king was exceedingly glad for him and commanded that Daniel be taken up out of the pit. So Daniel was taken up out of the pit, and no harm whatever was found on him, because he believed in his God. ²⁴ And the king commanded, and they brought those men who had slandered Daniel, and they cast them into the pit of lions—them, their children, and their wives—and before they reached the bottom of the pit, the lions overpowered them and broke all their bones to pieces.

Helpless before his own law, the king could only go **to his palace**, vanquished by his wily courtiers. There he **spent the night fasting**, not to implore divine mercy for Daniel, but in distress and mourning. **No diversions were brought before him**, as would have been customary. We cannot know what is meant by these customary **diversions**; some suggest music, dancing girls, or concubines. That night, however, the king spent in an agony of anxiety as **his sleep fled him**.

At first light he went in haste to the pit of lions. He cried out to Daniel, asking if his **God** had been **able to deliver** him **from the lions**. In good Jewish fashion, he refers to Daniel's god as **the living God** (compare the phrase in Deut. 5:26; Josh. 3:10; Ps. 42:2; Ps. 84:2; Is. 37:4; Jer. 10:10). Like a good storyteller, the narrator has kept the listener in suspense until now, and it is only when Daniel replies to his king, **"O king, live forever! My God sent His angel and shut the mouths of the lions, and they have not harmed me,"** that we learn of Daniel's fate. The God of Israel was indeed able to deliver Daniel from the lions, even as He was able to deliver his compatriots from the fiery furnace (3:15, 28). Daniel adds a protest of his own innocence, citing it as the reason God decided to deliver him: **innocence was found** in him—not just toward God, but also toward the king. His slanderers were unjust in portraying him as disloyal to his sovereign.

Daniel was immediately **taken up out of the pit** (probably with ropes) and checked out. It was as he said—the lions had not harmed him, and so **no harm was found** on his body. Not only had the lions not consumed him, they had not even touched him. Like the deliverance in the fiery furnace where the angel protected the three youths from any burn, so the angel sent to Daniel had protected him from a single scratch. The narrator stresses the cause again: Daniel was saved **because he believed in his God**. The lesson for future generations was clear: God will allow the faithful of all ages to tread safely on the lion if we trust Him (Ps. 91:13). We may safely lie in the midst of lions that greedily devour the sons of men. Though our enemies dig a pit for us, through God's mercy we will be rescued, while they will fall into it themselves (Ps. 57:4, 6).

The conclusion, though somewhat grisly to modern sensibilities, was satisfying to ancient ones. The Mosaic Law decreed that the fate intended by lying witnesses for their victims should be carried out on them (Deut. 19:18–19). Accordingly, the king had **those men who slandered Daniel cast into the pit of lions**—and not those men alone, but their entire families with them, including **their children and their wives**. The outrageousness of their behavior to the king coupled with an ancient understanding of family solidarity and corporate responsibility made such a sentence only just in ancient eyes.

To once again underscore the greatness of the deliverance, the narrator reports that the same lions that never touched Daniel were ferocious and hungry enough that **before** the victims **reached the bottom of the pit, the lions overpowered them and broke all**

their bones to pieces. Some have wondered about the logistics of throwing one hundred and twenty satraps along with their wives and children into a single pit, but the narrator is less concerned with historicity than with a satisfying and chilling ending to the story. Besides, as said above, it is unlikely that all the satraps of the kingdom were physically present and in on the plot.

> ²⁵ Then King Darius wrote, "To all peoples, nations, and languages that dwell in all the earth: Your peace be multiplied!
> ²⁶ I make a decree that in every dominion of my kingdom men tremble and fear before the God of Daniel,
>> for He is the living God,
>> enduring forever;
>> His kingdom is the one which shall not be destroyed,
>> and His dominion shall be to the end.
> ²⁷ He delivers and rescues,
>> and He works signs and wonders
>> in the heavens and in the earth,
>> who has delivered Daniel from the paw of the lions."
> ²⁸ So this Daniel prospered in the reign of Darius and in the reign of Cyrus the Persian.

Just as Nebuchadnezzar concluded his encounters with Daniel and his three friends by confessing the power of the Jewish God and by proclaiming as king that all in his empire should do likewise (2:47; 3:28–29; 4:34–35), so also Darius makes a similar proclamation. As Nebuchadnezzar decreed that all peoples, nations, and languages must refrain from blaspheming against the Jewish God (3:29), so Darius decrees that **all peoples, nations, and languages** should reverence Him (6:25f). Public acknowledgment of the Jewish God by the pagan kings is a theme of the Book of Daniel, and if not true as history, it is true as prophecy, for one day the kings of the earth would acknowledge the God of Israel through the proclamation of the Church's gospel.

Darius again refers to **the God of Daniel** in Jewish terms as **the living God, enduring forever**, and all but cites Psalm 145:13 when declaring that **His kingdom is the one which shall not be destroyed, and His dominion shall be to the end**. He is the One who works **signs and wonders** (see the note for 4:3). The message for the Jewish listener is plain: God **delivers and rescues**—not just Daniel, but all who trust in Him. He **delivered Daniel from the paw of the lions** (lit., "from the hand of the lions"), and He will deliver His servants from whatever distress they find themselves in, so long as, like Daniel, they defy impiety and persecution and maintain inner innocence of devotion to God (v. 22).

The story ends with an assurance that after this rescue **Daniel prospered**, continuing in peace and safety throughout **the reign of Darius** and into **the reign of Cyrus the Persian** (here portrayed as succeeding Darius as supreme ruler over Babylon).

THE ADVENTURES OF DANIEL AND HIS FRIENDS CLIMAX with this rescue from the pit of lions. Like all of the stories, it focuses upon the choice between faithfulness to God in the midst of a pagan land, on the one hand, and faithless abandonment of one's ancestral religion for the sake of advancement and assimilation on the other. This theme is central to every story. In chapter one, Daniel chose to push the boundaries of the culture in order to keep himself pure for God, despite the possible consequences. In chapter three, Daniel's companions refused to bow down to an idolatrous image, despite the threat of certain death if they held to their faith. In chapter five, Daniel again chose faithful devotion and prayer to God, even at the cost of being thrown to the lions.

At the back of all these stories, we may see not only the constant

experience of Israel scattered among the nations as a powerless diaspora, but also the shadow of Antiochus Epiphanes, oppressing the
Jews in their own land. Each of these tales gives the same counsel
and points to the same lesson—that God's people must resist the
temptation to abandon their faith and apostatize. They must remain
faithful to their ancestral faith, even in challenging circumstances.
Idolatrous diet, fiery furnace, or roaring lions, it is all one. The call
to steadfastness remains in all ages and in all circumstances.

We also saw in these stories the other abiding theme of God's
sovereignty over the nations. In chapter two, Nebuchadnezzar
received a vision declaring how all history lies in the hands of God,
who exalts and puts down kings and kingdoms as He wills. In
chapter four, we saw how Nebuchadnezzar's pride was punished by
God when he forgot this, and in chapter five, we saw how his "son"
Belshazzar's blasphemy was punished even more severely by Him.
The constant theme in all these stories is that the Jewish God reigns
over the nations of the earth and their kings. This is the common
refrain of both Daniel and the kings under whom he served (2:20–
22; 4:3, 34–35; 6:26–27), and it is the reason God's people should
remain faithful. He who reigns over the world knows what is in the
darkness (2:22); He sees all acts of infidelity to Him, as well as fidelity, and He is able to reward His servants when they cling to Him.

With the story of the deliverance from the pit of lions, the stories
of the Book of Daniel come to an end, but the wonders do not. The
next chapter opens with another dream—one given not to Nebuchadnezzar but to Daniel. Just as the mighty king had dreams and
visions (2:1; 4:5), so his Jewish subject and sage had dreams and
visions as well—a whole series of them, outlining the things God
had decreed for His world and His people.

The visions and dreams to follow, however, are not totally disconnected from the previous stories. They are all dated from the

reigns of the kings whose stories have been told, and the first vision builds on the dream given to Nebuchadnezzar in chapter two. In Nebuchadnezzar's dream, he saw an image composed of various metals and was told by Daniel that it meant four kingdoms would arise, the last of which would be smashed by supernatural means, and these kingdoms would be replaced by the Kingdom of God. The dream and its interpretation did not contain much detail about these kingdoms or the final smashing of them by divine power.

In the second half of the Book of Daniel, we find a series of visions that bring the meaning of that initial dream into progressively sharper focus as more and more details about coming events in the world are provided to Daniel. These details are provided by dreams, visions, and even by the appearances of angels. The adventure stories are over, but the eye-popping wonders have just begun.

PART III

The Visions of Daniel at the King's Court

The Vision of the Four Beasts
and the Man

JUST AS THE INTRODUCTORY STORY OF DANIEL'S REFUSAL TO eat the diet of idolatry in chapter one set the tone for the tales following it and prepared the listener for more stories about the importance of remaining faithful to God in the face of temptation, so this first vision of the future prepares the listener for more visions of the same. After the first story in chapter one, each story in chapters two to six returned to the same theme, reexamining it in ever greater detail and ever greater dramatic intensity. So it is with the visions: this first vision is foundational for all the visions that follow it, for those visions of chapters eight to twelve will return to examine this vision in ever greater detail.

The visions too will increase in intensity: first comes a dream in the night (chapter seven); then comes a vision in the daylight, explained by an angel (chapter eight); then comes a time of fasting and prayer followed by an angelic visitation in response (chapter nine); and finally another longer time of fasting is followed by an angelic visitation so overwhelming that Daniel falls down prostrate (chapters ten to twelve). The narrator has arranged the entire work with exquisite artistry.

7 ¹ In the first year of Belshazzar king of Babylon, Daniel had a dream and visions of his head while on his bed. Then he

wrote down the dream, telling the sum of the matter. ² Daniel spoke, saying, "I saw in my vision by night, and behold!—the four winds of heaven were stirring up the Great Sea. ³ And four great beasts came up out of the sea, each different from the others. ⁴ The first was like a lion and had eagle's wings. I watched till its wings were plucked off, and it was lifted up from the earth and made to stand on two feet like a man, and a man's heart was given to it. ⁵ And behold!—another beast, a second, like a bear. It was raised up on one side, and three ribs were in its mouth between its teeth. And thus they said to it: 'Arise, devour much flesh!' ⁶ After this I was looking, and behold!—there was another, like a leopard, with four wings of a bird on its back. The beast also had four heads, and dominion was given to it. ⁷ After this I saw in the night visions, and behold!—a fourth beast, terrible and frightening, exceedingly strong. It had huge iron teeth; it devoured, broke in pieces, and stamped the residue with its feet. It was different from all the beasts that were before it, and it had ten horns. ⁸ I considered the horns, and behold!—there was another horn, a little one, coming up among them, before whom three of the first horns were uprooted. And behold!—in this horn were eyes like the eyes of a man and a mouth speaking great things.

The narrator comes to his literary stage just long enough to date the coming dream, saying that it occurred **in the first year of Belshazzar king of Babylon**.[38] After this, Daniel takes the stage and speaks for himself in the first person for a greater sense of drama as he delivers **the sum of the matter** of a dream he had. By dating the dream to the first year of Belshazzar, the narrator returns the listener to the beginning and prepares him to revisit Daniel's career,

---

38   The four visions and revelations of chapters 7, 8, 9, and 10 are dated to the reigns of Belshazzar, Darius, and Cyrus, in chronological succession. This scheme of dating contributes to a sense of verisimilitude.

not by watching his adventures, but by listening to his accounts of visions. We here begin a new cycle in the life of Daniel.

The dream came as a true **vision** from God, a revelation that shook Daniel up, and it is not surprising that his recitation of the dream is punctuated by a series of six "behold!"s (vv. 2, 5, 6, 7, 8). Wonder succeeds wonder as the dream administers a series of visual shocks to sleeping Daniel.

Daniel begins by saying that he first saw **four winds of heaven stirring the Great Sea**. The term **the Great Sea** here is not simply a synonym for "a big ocean" but refers to the Mediterranean Sea (called "the Great Sea" by the ancients). That is, the Mediterranean world was being stirred and whipped up by all the providence of heaven, even as the four winds of the world stir up the sea. The image of the world scene as a tumultuous sea is a common one in the Scriptures, for the ancients thought of the sea as a threatening place, always in turmoil (compare Ps. 65:7; Is. 17:12; Jer. 6:23), a fit image for the turmoil of the nations and the changing of empires. The Great Sea therefore is here not simply the geographical body of water touching the borders of some of those empires; it is also an image of the primordial chaos, always pushing against the fragile order of the world and threatening to overwhelm it.

Not just one wind but all the **four winds of heaven** swept down on the sea and, **behold!**—(Daniel can hardly believe what he is seeing) turned it into a boiling tumult. And out of that tumult, Daniel saw **four great beasts** arise from the waters. One must appreciate the eerie aspect of the vision, since animals do not arise from the sea.

And these animals were like nothing ever seen. The first was **like a lion**. It was said to be "like" a lion, since it also **had eagle's wings**. Daniel **watched** in a kind of horrified fascination **till its wings were plucked off, and it was lifted up from the earth and made to stand on two feet like a man, and a man's heart was given**

to it. The lion symbolized Babylon—an easy identification since the four beasts clearly parallel the four kingdoms Nebuchadnezzar saw in his dream, and the first kingdom was the Babylonian one (2:38). The lion was an appropriate animal to represent Babylon, since images of a lion with eagle's wings abounded in Babylonian art. Jeremiah also spoke of Babylon as a lion (Jer. 4:7; 49:19; 50:44). The plucking off of the wings and standing the lion on two feet and giving it the mind of a man were all images for the humbling of Babylon's pride, imaged by the transformation of Nebuchadnezzar from beast to man narrated in chapter four.

As Daniel watched the vision, he received another shock (signaled by another **behold!**). Out of the sea came **another beast**, but not another lion—**a second, like a bear. It was raised up on one side, and three ribs were in its mouth between its teeth**, and it received the command (doubtless from God) **"Arise, devour much flesh!"** Bears are also mentioned often in the Scriptures along with lions as a source of danger (compare 1 Sam. 17:36; 2 Kin. 2:24; Prov. 28:15; Amos 5:19), and the bear was a fit image for a dangerous conquering people. The bear was presented as rearing up on its hind legs, the three ribs of a previous prey still sticking from its teeth. Not satisfied from its previous hunt, it was told to **devour much flesh**—a reference to the Medes' conquest of the large Babylonian empire, as prophesied (see Is. 13:17f; Jer. 51:11, 28).

Daniel continued looking, and another shocking wonder (signaled by **behold!**): there came **another** beast, **like a leopard with four wings on its back.** As well as having four wings for speed, it also had **four heads**, so that this animal was the strangest one yet. If the bear was Media, then the leopard symbolized Persia, famed for its speed in conquest just as the leopard was famed for its speed (Hab. 1:8). The four heads were the four kings of Persia mentioned in Daniel 11:2. According to the dream, **dominion was given to it**, for the Persian empire was geographically the largest of the ancient empires. Sovereignty over such a large area was said to be **given** to it, for all human sovereignty comes as the gift of God (compare Dan. 4:17).

Then came the sight of the fourth animal to emerge from the tossing waves. The shock of it was also introduced by a **behold!**, and yet Daniel could find no words to label the beast. It was unlike lion, bear, leopard, or any other named animal. Daniel could only describe it as **a fourth beast** and say that it was **terrible, frightening,** and **exceedingly strong**. It had **huge iron teeth,** and it **devoured, broke in pieces, and stamped the residue** of the other kingdoms into the dust **with its feet**. This beast was **different from all the beasts that were before it**. It was clearly the focus of the entire vision, and the rest of the vision would be spent in describing its progress (just as the description of the iron part of the statue in 2:40f occupied more time than the description of the other parts of the statue). With the fourth beast we come to the heart of the matter.

Daniel saw that, just as the other beasts were unnatural in having wings and more than one head, this beast also was unnatural and monstrous and **had ten horns** (in the Scriptures a horn symbolizes power; compare Ps. 75:10). Daniel **considered the horns**, looking in disconcerted fascination, and received another shock: there was **another horn, a little one, coming up among them, before whom three of the first horns were uprooted,** plucked out by their very roots. And more shocking and weird still, **in this horn were eyes like the eyes of a man and a mouth speaking great things**. Overfamiliarity with these words can perhaps blind us to how creepy the vision first appeared to Daniel.

9   "I watched till thrones were set up,
     and the ancient of days was seated;

his garment was white as snow,
and the hair of his head was like lamb's wool.
His throne was fiery flames,
its wheels a burning fire.

10 A river of fire issued
and came forth from before him.
A thousand thousands ministered to him;
ten thousand times ten thousand stood before him.
The court was seated,
and the books were opened.

11 I watched then because of the sound of the great words
which the horn was speaking. I watched till the beast was
slain, and its body destroyed and given to the burning
fire. 12 As for the rest of the beasts, they had their dominion
taken away, but their lives were prolonged for a season and
a time.

13 I was watching in the night visions,
And behold!—one like a son of man,
coming with the clouds of the heavens!
He came to the ancient of days,
and they brought him before him.

14 Then to him was given dominion and glory and a kingdom,
that all peoples, nations, and languages should serve him.
His dominion is an everlasting dominion,
which shall not pass away,
and his kingdom the one
which shall not be destroyed.

Unable to turn away, Daniel **watched till thrones were set up**. The setting up of a throne in ancient times always referred to a conqueror establishing his rule (compare Jer. 43:10). It seems as if the place of the setting up of the throne was on earth, not heaven (for if the one on the throne was God, His throne would already be set up in heaven). A conqueror had come! Though mention is made of **thrones** in the plural (seats ready for the court to assemble, v. 10), the main focus was on one who was **ancient of days** (i.e., very old)—so old and venerable that **the hair of his head** was white, **like lamb's wool**, and his **garment** also was **white as snow**, of spotless purity.

His **throne** was different from the others. It was **fiery flames**, and **its wheels**, like the wheels of a chariot, were also **a burning fire**. Not only that, **a river of fire issued and came forth from before him**. Who could dare to approach such a fearsome throne, such a terrible conflagration? Such was the power of this white-clad old man that **a thousand thousands ministered to him** and **ten thousand times ten thousand stood before him** ready to do his will. The time came, and **the court was seated, and the books** containing a record of the deeds of men (compare Ps. 56:8; 109:14; Is. 65:6) **were opened**. Judgment was at hand. But who was to be judged?

Daniel kept on looking, drawn to **the sound of the great words which the horn was speaking**. The words of boasting drew the wrath of the judge and the condemnation of his court, for the entire **beast** containing the boasting little horn **was slain and its body given to the burning fire** that proceeded from the throne. The other three **beasts**, however, were not touched; their **dominion** was **taken away**, but **their lives** could go on for a while.

Daniel scarcely had time to take in the sight when he received yet another shock: he kept **watching,** and then one like a human being (lit., **a son of man**; see such a use of the term in Ps. 8:4; Ezek. 2:1) was **coming with the clouds of the heavens.** If the throne of the ancient of days was indeed set up on earth, then the reference to the man **coming with the clouds** means that he was brought supernaturally from the ends of the earth. Despite the inferno engulfing the throne, he boldly **came to the ancient of days** seated there and was **brought before him**.

The ancient king on the throne bestowed upon the man a gift of unimagined sovereignty—**dominion, glory, and a kingdom** such that **all peoples, nations, and languages** would **serve him**. Indeed, his dominion was to be **an everlasting dominion, which shall not pass away, and his kingdom the one which shall not be destroyed**. This was no mere human empire, but the very Kingdom of God, for the words used to describe the kingdom of the one like a son of man were the very words used previously to describe God's eternal Kingdom (4:3, 34; 6:26). Surely, as Daniel now realized, the old man in white on the throne was the Lord of Hosts Himself.

[15] "As for me, Daniel, my spirit within me was grieved, and the visions of my head alarmed me. [16] I came near to one of those who stood by and asked him the truth concerning all this. So he told me and made known to me the interpretation of these things: [17] 'These great beasts, which are four, are four kings which shall arise out of the earth. [18] But the saints of the Most High shall receive the kingdom and possess the kingdom forever and ever.' [19] Then I desired to know the truth about the fourth beast, which was different from all of them, very frightening, with its teeth of iron and its claws of bronze, which devoured, broke in pieces, and stamped the residue with its feet, [20] and the ten horns that were on its head, and the other horn that came up, before which three fell, namely, that horn which had eyes and a mouth that spoke great things, whose appearance was greater than his fellows. [21] I was watching; and the same horn was making war against the saints and prevailed over them, [22] until the Ancient of Days came, and a judgment was given for the saints of the Most High, and the time came when the saints possessed the kingdom.

²³ Thus he said:
   'The fourth beast shall be
   a fourth kingdom on earth,
   which shall be different from all the other kingdoms,
   and shall devour the whole earth,
   trample on it and break it in pieces.
²⁴ The ten horns are ten kings
   who shall arise from this kingdom.
   And another shall rise after them;
   he shall be different from the previous ones,
   and shall put down three kings.
²⁵ He shall speak words against the Most High,
   and wear out the saints of the Most High,
   and shall intend to change times and law.
   And they shall be given into his hand
   for a time and times and half a time.
²⁶ But the court shall be seated,
   and they shall take away his dominion,
   to consume and destroy it to the end.
²⁷ Then the kingdom and dominion,
   and the greatness of the kingdoms under the whole heaven,
   shall be given to the people of the saints of the Most High.
   His kingdom is an everlasting kingdom,
   and all dominions shall serve and obey Him.'
²⁸ This is the end of the matter. As for me, Daniel, my thoughts
   greatly alarmed me, and my countenance changed; but I
   kept the matter in my heart."

At such a vision, Daniel's **spirit within was grieved**—that is, he was shaken to his core.[39] As Nebuchadnezzar once needed Daniel's divine assistance to understand his dream, so now Daniel requires

---

39   The Aramaic literally reads, "my spirit in its sheath," i.e., within his body.

such help to understand his. He therefore **came near to one of those who stood by** (doubtless one of the angelic retainers waiting on the Ancient of Days) and asked for the meaning of the dream. He was told the great beasts were **four kings** (i.e., kingdoms) **which shall arise out of the earth,**[40] whose rule will be replaced by the rule of **the saints of the Most High,** so that these saints will **possess the kingdom forever and ever**. The **one like a son of man** was therefore an image of the saints, even as the four beasts were symbols of the four kingdoms.

The contrast is clear: just as the kingdoms considered were brutal, bestial, irrational, and cruel, so the coming kingdom of the Most High would be kind, intelligent, upright, and in the image of God. As a human being is more exalted than a beast, so is the coming kingdom superior to those that preceded it. That was why the kingdom of the saints has as its symbol a human being, a son of man.

Never again, therefore, after **the saints receive the kingdom** of God, will merely human kingdoms reign on earth. Tyrants might rule the earth in weary and bloody succession, but one day God will intervene and bring in His own rule. That was the main message of the vision, but with such a wealth of eerie detail, Daniel naturally wanted to know more about **the fourth beast, which was different** from all its predecessors, and had **ten horns**, and the **other** little **horn** with **eyes** and a boastful **mouth**.

The **fourth beast** symbolized the Macedonian or Greek empire of Alexander the Great. As we have seen above, this was the view of the Sibyl (dating from about 140 BC). It is also reflected in 2 Esdras 12:11–12, written in the first century. Since the author of 2 Esdras suffered under the Roman Empire, he wanted to apply this

---

40   In v. 3 Daniel saw in his vision the beasts arise out of "the sea," but here in its interpretation they are said to "arise out of the earth," for the sea was but a symbol of the Mediterranean world.

prophecy of Daniel to his own time and so make Daniel's fourth beast a symbol of Rome. But even he says, "The eagle which you saw coming up from the sea is the fourth kingdom which appeared in a vision to our brother Daniel. But it was not explained to him as I now explain it to you"—in other words, the author admits that before his time the identity of the fourth beast was not considered to be the Roman Empire, but the Greek one. This was also the view of St. Ephraim the Syrian and of the Peshitta version of the Book of Daniel, the classic Syriac version of the Bible.

It was fitting that the fourth beast should be described in such terrifying terms and as having **stamped the residue** of the kingdoms **with its feet**, for Alexander's conquest astonished the world. It was **different from all** the others, because it was the first non-oriental power to conquer the Near East. His kingdom ultimately gave rise, after his untimely death at the age of thirty-two, to the Seleucid and Ptolemaic kingdoms of Syria and Egypt, respectively, called in Daniel 11 "the king of the north" and "the king of the south."

The **ten horns** are the kings of the Seleucid kingdom. The number ten might well be a round number to indicate the kings of that regime which so tyrannized Israel, but by the **three** horns something specific seems to be meant. Complete certainty is elusive, but one possibility is that the three represent the father of Seleucus IV of the Seleucids and his two sons, for these were in the immediate line of succession before Antiochus IV. These **kings** he **put down** and supplanted to become the next king (vv. 20, 24). There is little doubt that the little horn represents Antiochus IV Epiphanes ("God Manifest"), a title Jews twisted to Antiochus *Epimanes*—Antiochus "the Madman."

Antiochus Epiphanes did indeed **make war against the** Jewish **saints** in Palestine and **prevailed over them**. In 1 Maccabees we read of him embarking on a program of Hellenization in Israel

(1 Macc. 1:11–15). But more than that, Antiochus entered the sanctuary of the temple and plundered its holy vessels. When resistance arose in Israel, he embarked on another program of forced conversion, forbidding temple sacrifices, forbidding Jews to keep the Sabbath and the feasts, forbidding circumcision, and enforcing the sacrifice of swine. In 167 BC he erected the abomination of desolation in the temple and burned any copies of the Law he could find. Those found in possession of the Law were condemned to death (1 Macc. 1:41f). Such savage persecution solely for the practice of one's ancestral religion was unheard of in Israel and, in fact, in the world. Antiochus was also the first Hellenistic monarch to make a claim to divinity; some of the coins he had issued bore the words "King Antiochus, God Manifest [Gr. *Epiphanous*]" on them.

These outrages are characterized in the vision as **speaking words against the Most High** and **wearing out the saints of the Most High**, the saints being the pious Jews who clung to their ancestral faith and suffered for it. Antiochus by his decrees **intended to change times and law**, altering and forbidding the Jewish calendar and Sabbaths, and the other commandments and provisions of the Torah. And he succeeded, for things were **given into his hand** by God, but only for **a time, times, and half a time**. By "a time" is meant "a year" (compare Dan. 4:16), so that "a time" equals a year, "times" equals two years, and "half a time" equals six months, for a total of three and a half years. This is the approximate time of Antiochus's ascendency, from the temple's desecration in 167 BC to its purification in 164 BC. The phrase is symbolic and refers to the agonizing lengthening of the suffering, followed by the sudden and merciful cutting short of that terrible period in Jewish history. (More precise numbers for the persecution and cessation of temple sacrifices will be given in the visions to come, as the visions progressively increase in fine detail.)

The divine court will intervene. The **court shall be seated** to render its verdict and to execute its sentence. They shall take away his dominion to consume and destroy it to the end. Antiochus and his empire will be delivered to a final fiery destruction. The lands of Babylon, Media, and Persia will continue for a while (v. 12), but the fourth kingdom will be annihilated. In its place, **the greatness of the kingdoms under the whole heaven** will be **given to the people of the saints of the Most High**. God will rule the earth through His people, offering peace and tranquility. The word will go forth from Zion, and all the nations will resort to God's House in Palestine that He might teach them His ways (Is. 2:2f). The wolf will lie down with the lamb, and the earth will be full of the knowledge of the Lord as the waters cover the sea (Is. 11:6–9). That **kingdom** will be **an everlasting kingdom**, and it will come through the supernatural power of God as soon as the power of the little horn is broken.

With this angelic explanation, Daniel concludes the recitation of his dream. One senses his exhaustion and how overwhelmed he was to receive a revelation of such import. Though his **thoughts greatly alarmed** him so that his **countenance changed** (with all the blood draining from his face as he turned pale), he did not run out to tell everyone. Rather he **kept the matter in** his **heart**. (In fact, we later learn, after receiving even more of these visions, he decided to seal them up to keep them secret for years; compare 12:9).

WHAT ARE WE TO MAKE OF ALL THIS TODAY? Final reflections, including Christological ones, will come at the conclusion, but here a few preliminary reflections may be offered.

As we begin to examine the visions of Daniel, it is important that we hear the narrative as it was meant to be heard—that is, with wide-eyed wonder. It is too easy to approach the visions as students, regarding them as so many puzzles to be solved and pieces to be fitted together. Which kingdom is represented by the fourth beast—Greece or Rome? Is the little horn in chapter seven the same little horn as in chapter eight? Which date do we use to start counting the seventy weeks? Is there a gap in the counting of the week? Are we still talking about Antiochus Epiphanes at the end of chapter eleven?

These are not unimportant questions, but they should not be allowed to elbow out the main fact about these visions, which is that they are exciting. A child looking at them (which is to say, anyone looking at them properly) would notice first of all not these questions but the fact that these realities come in mysterious and amazing ways. Daniel has a scary dream. Then he has a vision in broad daylight which somehow transports him to a faraway place. Then he meets an angel. Then he fasts and receives another visit from an angel. Then he fasts for an even longer time and gets a visit from an angel so overpowering that he collapses and needs the angel to help him to his knees. The wonders and miracles encountered in the stories continue apace with recounting of the visions.

This first and foundational vision begins with a storytelling bang, presenting the listener with a nightmare filled with monstrous animals, including a horn that sees and speaks and does terrible things. The picture suddenly switches to a throne, inhabited by a venerable figure clad all in white, sitting in the midst of an inferno with untold thousands waiting upon him. Judgment is passed on the last animal, the one with the horrible little horn, and it is destroyed and consigned to the flames. Then a man comes with the clouds, brought supernaturally to the throne from the earth's end, and receives all the power in the world as the inheritor of the eternal Kingdom of God. It is a stupendous story all by itself. Before there was *Star Wars,* there was the Book of Daniel.

In our explanation offered here (to be examined in greater depth later), the four beasts are Assyria/Babylon, Media, Persia, and Macedonia/Greece, with its final manifestation in Palestine under the Seleucids, and the little horn is Antiochus Epiphanes. His significance for Israel in the second century before Christ can scarcely be exaggerated. For the first time in their existence, God's people experienced not just disaster such as exile, but persecution in their own land solely because of their faithfulness to God. This persecution produced a trauma which hardly healed (the establishment of the feast of Hanukkah was one attempt at healing).

At that time, the faithful in the land desperately required encouragement. They had returned to Palestine after the Babylonian exile and had slowly and painfully rebuilt their national existence. They had their temple back (though on a greatly reduced scale; see Ezra 3:12) and a measure of security under foreign rulers. With the exile behind them and no idolatry thriving in the land as before, they thought the road ahead was clear and there was nothing to fear. God had promised through His prophets there would be security after they returned from Babylon, and everlasting joy would rest on their heads like a crown (Is. 51:11). With the persecution of Antiochus, it seemed as if their dream had turned into a nightmare. Everything was wrong, and the world was somehow spinning out of control. What happened to God's promises? How could He just let Antiochus blaspheme His Name, defile His altar, burn His Torah, and terrorize His saints?

This vision, and the following ones that fill out the details, gives the answer. God still reigns in heaven, directing the course of history. He is still the One who changes times and seasons and removes kings and sets up kings (Dan. 2:21). He has seen Antiochus's mischief and will take it into His hand to set it right (Ps. 10:14). On the ashes of the worst tyranny and evil, He will establish His eternal

Kingdom and vindicate His people so that the man who is of the earth may cause terror no more (Ps. 10:18).

The Jews of the second century BC thought the worst thing that could ever happen was Antiochus IV. With him, history had reached its nadir, and they were tempted to believe God's promises had failed. The visions provide God's answer to the Jews: His promises had not failed, but He would indeed destroy evil and bring in His Kingdom. The faithful in Israel should not despair or apostatize. Let them hold to their faith, even to the death if need be, and wait for the delivering hand of the Most High.

DANIEL 8

The Vision of the Ram
and the He-goat

IN THIS VISION WE FOCUS MORE CLOSELY ON THE FIGURE OF the little horn. As the previous parts of the Book of Daniel (from chapter two to the end of chapter seven) were in Aramaic, so here we switch back into Hebrew.[41] If we are correct in suggesting that chapter one (in Hebrew) introduces the rest of the adventure stories (in Aramaic), then we note here a similar pattern of chapter seven (in Aramaic) introducing the rest of the visions (in Hebrew). In other words the switch here from Aramaic to Hebrew may be for reasons of stylistic parallelism and chiasmus, so that the pattern through the Book of Daniel is one of Hebrew–Aramaic–Aramaic–Hebrew.

Just as the initial switch from Hebrew to Aramaic served to increase the listener's sense of listening in at a foreign court, so the switch here from Aramaic to Hebrew serves another literary purpose. These visions focus largely on the struggle between the aggressive Hellenism and persecution of Antiochus Epiphanes on one hand and the pious traditionalists of Israel on the other. Presenting the visions in the holy Hebrew language, the ancestral tongue of Israel, serves to anchor the listener on the side of the traditionalists, accenting the difference between the Hellenists and the faithful.

---

41 Some scholars suggest that the Hebrew is of inferior quality to the Aramaic, suggesting that the author was more at home in the latter than the former, and that this also witnesses to a late date.

8 ¹ In the third year of the reign of King Belshazzar, a vision appeared to me—to me, Daniel—after the one that appeared to me at the first. ² I looked in the vision, and it happened while I was looking that I was in Susa, the citadel, which is in the province of Elam; and I saw in the vision that I was by the Ulai Canal. ³ Then I lifted my eyes and saw, and behold!—standing beside the canal was a ram which had two horns, and the two horns were high; but one was higher than the other, and the higher one came up last. ⁴ I looked at the ram butting westward, northward, and southward, so that no animal could stand before him; nor was there any that could deliver from his hand, but he did according to his will and became great. ⁵ And as I was considering, behold!—a he-goat came from the west, across the surface of the whole earth, without touching the ground; and the goat had a conspicuous horn between his eyes. ⁶ Then he came to the ram that had two horns, which I had seen standing beside the canal, and ran at him with furious power. ⁷ And I saw him come close to the ram; he was enraged against him, struck the ram, and broke his two horns. There was no power in the ram to stand before him, but he cast him down to the ground and trampled him; and there was no one that could deliver the ram from his hand. ⁸ Therefore the he-goat became very great; but when he became strong, the large horn was broken, and in place of it four conspicuous ones came up toward the four winds of the heavens. ⁹ And out of one of them came a little horn which grew exceedingly great toward the south, toward the east, and toward the Beautiful Land. ¹⁰ And it grew great, even to the host of the heavens; and it cast down some of the host and some of the stars to the earth and trampled them. ¹¹ He even exalted himself as high as the Prince of the host; and by him the daily sacrifice was taken away, and the place of His sanctuary was cast down. ¹² Because of transgression, a host was given over to the horn with the daily sacrifice; and he cast truth down to the ground. He did all this and prospered. ¹³ Then I heard a certain holy one

speaking; and another holy one said to that one who was speaking, "How long will the vision be, concerning the daily sacrifice and the transgression of desolation, the giving of both the sanctuary and the host to be trampled underfoot?" [14] And he said to me, "For two thousand three hundred evenings and mornings; then the sanctuary shall be restored."

This vision is dated two years after the first, **in the third year of the reign of King Belshazzar**. It is explicitly linked to **the one that appeared to me at the first** (i.e., in chapter 7), preparing us for more details about that first vision. There is a difference between the two, however, for the previous vision occurred through a dream during the night (7:1), but this one took place during the day.

Daniel was, of course, still in Babylon, attached as he was to the court of Belshazzar. But he **looked** and **in** his **vision** was transported to **Susa, the citadel** or fortified city **in the province of Elam**. That is, he was mystically present two hundred miles east of Babylon, for Elam was situated between Babylon and Persia, to the north of the Persian Gulf. Daniel's experience therefore paralleled that of Ezekiel, for when Ezekiel was in Babylon, he was mystically transported back to Jerusalem in a vision (Ezek. 8:1–4). That is, though physically present in Babylon, Ezekiel was able to see in a vision things occurring elsewhere.

Daniel related that he was **by the Ulai Canal**, perhaps hearkening back to Ezekiel's revelation of the Chebar River (Ezek. 1:3). Why was Daniel transported in a vision to Susa? For he could have had the vision in any place. But it was appropriate that he stand mystically in the very place of the struggle he would soon witness in a vision, for the vision had to do with the contest between the Medo-Persian Empire (represented by the fortified city of Susa) and the growing Greek threat of Alexander the Great. Daniel therefore was transported away from Babylon (which was far from the center of future action) to the site of the coming struggle between the superpowers.

Standing by the place of revelation, he beheld **a ram which had two horns**, both of which were **high**, but the **one** that **came up last** was **higher**. Both the ram and the he-goat are apt images of power, and they are often found together in the Scriptures (e.g., Ezek. 34:17). Leaders are sometimes referred to as he-goats (e.g., Is. 14:9: "Sheol stirs up the dead to meet you, all the leaders [lit., 'he-goats'] of the earth"; Zech. 10:3: "My anger is kindled against the shepherds and I punished the leaders [lit., 'he-goats']).

The ram in the vision began **butting westward, northward, and southward**, with **no animal** able to **stand before him**. With such invincibility the ram conquered whatever he wanted to and **became great**. The ram symbolized the power of the Medes and the Persians, and its two horns the Median and Persian kings, respectively. Cyrus the Great was at first a vassal to the Medes but rebelled against them, defeated them in 550 BC, and incorporated them into his Persian Empire—thus the second horn of the Medo-Persian empire coming up **higher**, for the Persians grew mightier than the Medes. As Persia was the furthest east of the empires in Israel's world, the narrator views its expansion primarily as reaching **westward, northward, and southward**.

The shock of seeing a ram with two unequal horns (thus the surprise expressed in **behold!** in v. 3) was compounded by the sight of another animal (with another **behold!** in v. 5). Daniel saw a **he-goat**, which was astounding because it came racing **from the west** so quickly that its feet did not even **touch the ground**, and **between his eyes** he had an unusually large and **conspicuous horn**. The ram no animal could withstand and which had proven invincible proved no match for the he-goat. The he-goat **ran** at the ram **with** such **furious power** that he **broke his two horns**. The ram was finished; the he-goat **cast him to the ground and**

trampled him with impunity. Then, as the ram had done before him, the he-goat too **became very great**. Then another shock—just when the he-goat **became strong**, the **large horn was broken, and in place of it four conspicuous ones came up**, pointing not in the same direction (as animal horns might be expected to do), but rather **toward the four winds of the heavens**.

It would take the ancients no imagination to understand the vision, even apart from angelic help. The **he-goat** was clearly the Macedonian or Greek Empire, and the **conspicuous horn**, Alexander the Great. He conquered the world with such speed that indeed it seemed that he ran **across the surface of the whole earth without touching the ground**. He conquered the Medo-Persian Empire as he conquered everything else, and his dominion stretched from Greece to India. The death of Alexander at the height of his power, the time when **the large horn was broken**, shocked the world. After this, his empire was divided among four of his generals, whose authority was indeed scattered everywhere like **the four winds of the heavens**. One ruled Macedonia and Greece; another ruled Asia Minor; another Syria, Babylonia, and the East; and another Egypt.

The vision has only peripheral interest in the contest of these superpowers, and it hurries on to its real concern, the battle of the **little horn** with the people of God. He is described as coming out of the four horns (i.e., from the horn ruling Syria, Babylonia, and the East) and as growing **exceedingly great toward the south** (Egypt), **toward the east** (Parthia), **and toward the Beautiful Land** (Palestine). The **little horn**, Antiochus Epiphanes, **grew great, even to the host of the heavens**, exalting himself as a god. His hubris achieved mythical proportions, so that he even **cast down some of the host and some of the stars to the earth, and trampled them**. Antiochus ignored the gods of his fathers and successfully exalted himself above them all, so that he magnified himself above every god (Dan.

11:36–37). Like the Daystar, the king of Babylon before him, the **little horn** thought to ascend to heaven, above the stars of God, and to make himself like the Most High (Is. 14:13–14). He arrogantly defied both God's angels and pagan deities, fearing no one.

More scandalous still, he even exalted himself **as high as the Prince of the host** of heaven, as high as Yahweh Himself, for **by him the daily sacrifice** (Heb. *tamid*) **was taken away, and the place of His sanctuary cast down**. Because of the **transgression** and apostasy of many in Israel, Antiochus was allowed to **prosper**. He successfully triumphed over **the host** of heaven, deifying himself as God Manifest; he removed **the daily sacrifice**, the burnt offering made each evening and morning, and **cast truth to the ground**, forcing Jews to abandon the covenant, refrain from circumcision, and burn the Torah.

Such outrages were too much to be endured, and the ancient cry went up from one of the holy ones, **"How long?"** (compare Ps. 74:10; 79:5; 80:4) How long before the **daily sacrifice** is restored, and the temple cleansed of the **transgression of desolation** that defiled it, and the heavenly **host** avenged?

The answer came from another angel as Daniel listened to their heavenly exchange: **"For two thousand three hundred evenings and mornings; then the sanctuary shall be restored."** The figure 2300 refers not to 2300 days, but to 2300 "evening-mornings"— that is, 2300 offerings of the daily sacrifice (Heb. *tamid*), or 1150 days. This amounts to just slightly more than the time between the desecration of the temple and its rededication. The ancients were less interested in precision than we are and more appreciative of symbols.

> [15] Then it was, when I, Daniel, had seen the vision and was seeking the meaning, behold!—the appearance of a man stood before me. [16] And I heard a man's voice between the banks of the Ulai,

who called and said, "Gabriel, make this one understand the vision." ¹⁷ So he came near beside me, and when he came I was afraid and fell on my face; but he said to me, "Understand, son of man, that the vision refers to the time of the end." ¹⁸ Now, as he was speaking with me, I was in a deep sleep with my face to the earth; but he touched me and set me upright. ¹⁹ And he said, "Behold, I am making known to you what shall happen in the last time of the indignation; for at the appointed time the end shall be. ²⁰ The ram which you saw, having the two horns—they are the kings of Media and Persia. ²¹ And the he-goat is the kingdom of Greece. The great horn between its eyes is the first king. ²² As for the broken horn and the four that stood up in its place, four kingdoms shall arise out of the nation, but not with its power.

²³ And in the last time of their kingdom,
   when the transgressors have come to the full,
   a king shall arise,
   strong of face,
   skilled at intrigues.
²⁴ His power shall be great,
   he shall destroy fearfully,
   and shall prosper in what he does;
   he shall destroy the mighty, and also the holy people.
²⁵ Through his cunning
   he shall cause deceit to prosper under his hand,
   and he shall lift himself up in his heart.
   He shall destroy many at ease.
   He shall even rise against the Ruler of rulers,
   but he shall be broken without human hand.
²⁶ And the vision of the evenings and mornings
   which was told is true.
   Therefore seal up the vision,
   for it refers to many days hence."
²⁷ And I, Daniel, was faint and sick for days; then I rose and went

about the king's business. I was astonished by the vision but did not understand it.

After this vision, another shock—**behold!**—**the appearance of a man** [Heb. *geber*] **stood before** Daniel. Daniel **heard a man's voice** (i.e., the voice of the angel, who had the appearance of a man) from **between the banks of the Ulai,** standing above the waters of the canal (compare 12:6) and ordering that the interpretation of the vision be made known. The **man** named here is the angel **Gabriel**—doubtless containing a play on words, for the name Gabriel means "man [Heb. *geber*] of God." The word *geber* means not just "man," but "manly, athletic, heroic, a champion"—an apt name for an archangel. In Psalm 19:5 it is translated as "strong man" (NASB) and even as "giant" (NAB). Overwhelmed and fearful at the vision, Daniel **fell on** his **face** and collapsed as if in a **deep sleep**, and needed help from the angel before he could stand **upright**. Daniel's detailed reaction to the vision was no mere filler but shows how important the events are in Israel's history.

The angel explained the opening part of the vision describing Media, Persia, and Greece quickly enough, hurrying on to the important part that concerned Israel directly, narrating it in poetry rather than prose as a sign of its importance. In **the last time of** the **kingdom** of the Greeks, **when the transgressors have come to the full,** then a certain **king shall arise**, Antiochus Epiphanes, the **little horn** who will devastate Israel and persecute its pious ones. The angel revealed that such outrages were only permitted because the apostates in Israel, the Hellenizers, **the transgressors**, had departed from their ancestral ways and cooperated with the new king. We have here, therefore, a less-than-subtle attack on the Hellenization that was sweeping through the ancient world of that time.

The king is described as **strong of face** (i.e., bold and brazen) and **skilled at intrigues** (duplicity and doubletalk), so that he both openly and covertly pushes his godless agenda. He **destroys** both **the mighty** pagan forces of his foes **and also the holy people**, the Jews. He **destroys** those **who are at peace**, falling upon them suddenly and unexpectedly, as in the unprovoked attack against Jerusalem referred to in 1 Maccabees 1:29–33.

Such attacks on God's people constituted an assault against God Himself, **the Ruler of rulers**. God would avenge such bold defiance, and the **little horn** would **be broken without human hand**, falling by the outstretched hand of the Most High Himself. Antiochus's sudden sickness and untimely death soon after in 164 BC were interpreted as just such a judgment. After the interpretation, the angel assures Daniel that the vision was true and therefore assured of fulfillment, and that Antiochus's fate was fixed. Daniel must therefore **seal up the vision**, sharing it with no one until closer to the time of fulfillment, **many days hence** (compare 12:9).

Daniel concludes his narration by sharing that after such an overwhelming revelation, he was **faint and sick for days**; it was only after he recovered that he could return to some sense of normalcy and go **about the king's business**. The first vision had been exhausting (7:28), but this was even worse, for the revelations were growing in intensity and importance.

Daniel ends by admitting that he **did not understand the vision**. The subtext of this final statement is clear: the events concerned things so far off that they made no sense to Daniel at that time. By adding this, the author of the Book of Daniel makes his point that the vision was given long before the predicted events, adding to a sense of prophetic verisimilitude.

THE VISION OF THE RAM AND THE HE-GOAT FILLS IN MORE details, steeling the people of God to resist the temptation to apostatize under Antiochus Epiphanes (or under anyone else). The practical lessons of perseverance are therefore substantially the same as the ones offered in chapter seven. But the extra details provided here offer extra lessons as well.

In particular, we may examine the detail about the 2300 evening-mornings. Some scholars have suggested that the figure indeed represents 2300 days, each day containing an evening-morning, a *tamid* sacrifice in the evening and in the morning. This figure is problematic, for then the total number of days would be six or seven years, which is much longer than the period during which the temple remained defiled. It seems best to accept the view that the figure represents 2300 different *tamid*s spread over 1150 days.

This view allows us to view each *tamid*, each daily sacrifice, as precious and important. The vision counts each and every one of them, viewing the loss of any one as a new and separate tragedy. We see here the importance of the evening offering and the morning offering (put in this order because the day was thought of as beginning in the evening; compare Gen. 1:5: "There was evening and there was morning, one day"). Sacrifice was the way a worshipper communed and drew near to deity, both in Israel and elsewhere, which is why the loss of the temple was felt so keenly during the exile. God in His Law mandated that Israel draw near through sacrifice every evening and every morning, living in constant communion with Him (Ex. 29:38–39).

In the same way, we Christians should draw near to God in the evening and in the morning, both ending and beginning the day with prayer to God, offering the sacrifice of praise. A day devoid of such a spiritual *tamid* is a day lost, a tragedy. The pain felt in the vision at the loss of the 2300 sacrifices teaches us to stand before the Lord as part of His holy royal priesthood and offer spiritual sacrifices acceptable to God through Jesus Christ (1 Pet. 2:5).

DANIEL 9

The Vision of the Seventy Weeks

9 ¹In the first year of Darius the son of Ahasuerus, of the seed of the Medes, who was made king over the kingdom of the Chaldeans— ² in the first year of his reign I, Daniel, understood by the books the number of the years which came as the word of Yahweh through Jeremiah the prophet, that He would accomplish seventy years for the desolation of Jerusalem.

The next vision does not come unbidden as did the first two (7:1; 8:1), but as a result of fervent prayer to God. It is dated to **the first year of Darius the son of Ahasuerus**[42]—the year that Babylon fell to Darius the Mede. (Babylon is here styled **the kingdom of the Chaldeans**, since Belshazzar was called "the Chaldean king" in Dan. 5:30.) At the fall of Babylon, Daniel **understood by the books**[43] **the number of the years which came as the word of Yahweh through Jeremiah the prophet, that He would accomplish seventy years for the desolation of Jerusalem**. That is, Daniel could tell by looking at the Scriptures of the prophets that God had

---

42   The historical Darius I was not the son of Ahasuerus ("Xerxes" in the Greek) but his father. It is possible that the narrator made Ahasuerus the father of Darius through a mistaken reading of Ezra 4:6, 24, which mentions Ahasuerus before Darius.

43   We note here another anachronism, for reference to "the books" presupposes a canonical collection of prophetic literature, which collection did not yet exist during the exile. The words of Jeremiah were not yet considered "the books" or "the Scriptures" at the time of the Babylonian captivity.

foretold Jerusalem would lie in **desolation** for **seventy years** and after this would be restored.

What was this **word of Yahweh through Jeremiah the prophet**? It seems to refer to such utterances as found in Jeremiah 25:11f: "This whole land [of Judah] shall become a ruin and a waste, and these nations shall serve the king of Babylon seventy years. Then after seventy years are completed, I will punish the king of Babylon and that nation." Also Jeremiah 29:4f: "To all the exiles whom I have sent into exile from Jerusalem to Babylon: build houses and live in them; plant gardens and eat their produce . . . seek the welfare of the city where I have sent you into exile. . . . When seventy years are completed for Babylon, I will visit you, and I will fulfill to you My promise to bring you back to this place [Jerusalem]."

These words were spoken by Jeremiah in 605 and 597, respectively. Both said the Babylonian captivity would last seventy years. The term "seventy years" should be understood generally as meaning a lifetime (compare Ps. 90:10), so that those exiled in Jeremiah's time should not look for a quick return as was promised by the false prophets (see Jer. 28:1–4). The figure should not be unduly pressed for exactitude—especially since historical exactitude was foreign to ancient ways of thinking for the common man.

³ Then I set my face toward the Lord God to seek Him by prayer and supplications, with fasting, sackcloth, and ashes. ⁴ And I prayed to Yahweh my God, and made confession, and said, "O Lord, great and awesome God, who keeps His covenant and loving-kindness with those who love Him, and with those who keep His commandments, ⁵ we have sinned and done iniquity, we have done wickedly and rebelled, turning aside from Your commandments and Your judgments. ⁶ We have not listened to Your servants the prophets, who spoke in Your name to our kings and our princes, to our fathers and all the people of the land. ⁷ O Lord, to You

belongs righteousness, but to us shame of face, as it is this day—to the men of Judah, to the inhabitants of Jerusalem and all Israel, those near and those far away in all the lands to which You have scattered them, because of the unfaithfulness which they have done against You. [8] O Lord, to us belongs shame of face, to our kings, our princes, and our fathers, because we have sinned against You. [9] To the Lord our God belong mercy and forgiveness, for we have rebelled against Him. [10] We have not obeyed the voice of Yahweh our God, to walk in His laws, which He set before us by His servants the prophets. [11] All Israel has transgressed Your Law and turned aside, not obeying Your voice; therefore the curse and the oath written in the Law of Moses the servant of God have been poured out on us, because we have sinned against Him. [12] And He has confirmed His words, which He spoke against us and against our judges who judged us, by bringing upon us a great evil; for under the whole heaven there has not been done the like of what has been done to Jerusalem. [13] As it is written in the Law of Moses, all this evil has come upon us. Because we did not entreat the favor of Yahweh our God, turning from our iniquities and giving heed to Your truth, [14] therefore Yahweh has kept ready the evil and brought it upon us, for Yahweh our God is righteous in all the works which He does, and we have not obeyed His voice.

Encouraged by Babylon's fall, Daniel **set** his **face to seek God** through fervent **prayer**, with penitential **fasting, sackcloth, and ashes,** that He would restore the holy city as He had promised. We see here that the words of the prophets were not given to Israel simply to be received passively as if they were a weather prediction. The prophets spoke not simply to impart fatalistic information but to elicit a response of repentance and faith (e.g., Jonah 3:4–5).

Daniel understood that the time for Jerusalem's devastation was due to end, saw that it still lay in ruins, and began to intercede and seek God's mercy. He did so emboldened by God's promise of the city's final restoration. Sometimes God's judgment is final, leaving no hope of recovery (such as, for example, his judgment on Babylon in Is. 13:19f: "Babylon . . . will be like Sodom and Gomorrah when God overthrew them. It will never be inhabited or lived in for all generations . . . no shepherds will make their flocks lie down there, but wild beasts will lie down there, and its houses will be full of howling creatures"). But it was otherwise with His judgment on Jerusalem; God had promised recovery, and it was on this basis that Daniel found courage to pray.

The intercession begins with a thorough confession of national sin, much like Ezra's confession of the people's sin found in Ezra 9 (and the Prayer of Azariah in the so-called "Additions to the Book of Daniel"). Daniel confesses that the calamity that has befallen Israel and Jerusalem and from which they pray to be delivered is entirely their own fault. God **keeps His covenant** and shows **lovingkindness** to **those who love Him**. The word rendered here **lovingkindness** is the Hebrew *hesed*, meaning "steadfast love, mercy, covenant loyalty." God is faithful to His covenant and reliable—if His people fulfill their part of the covenant, He will fulfill His part and will protect, bless, and save them. That was the essence of the covenant He made with His people at Sinai—He would be their God and take care of them, and they would be His people and love and serve no one but Him.

As with all such treaties and covenants in the ancient world, there were stipulated consequences if one broke and violated the covenant. Daniel refers to them here as **the curse and the oath written in the Law of Moses**. The covenant expressly declared that if Israel sinned against God, abandoning Him for other gods and breaking His Law, then a multitude of disasters would be **poured out** on them, culminating in Israel being besieged, defeated, and scattered among all people, from one end of the earth to the other

(Deut. 28:49–57, 64). Indeed, Israel had sinned and had reaped the promised judgment for their disobedience.

It is these sins and this rebellion that Daniel confesses on behalf of his people. Over and over again, he acknowledges that **to** God **belongs righteousness** and to Israel **shame of face**. They heartily deserve all the catastrophe and disgrace that have engulfed them. Through **His servants the prophets,** God warned the entire nation from top to bottom—their **kings**, their **princes**, their **fathers**, and **all the** humble **people of the land**—and yet the whole nation, **all Israel**, still **rebelled against Him** and **transgressed** His **Law**. Therefore God **confirmed His words** of threatened judgment **which He spoke against** Israel and its **judges** and rulers by **bringing upon** them the **great evil** and disaster—a disaster so great that **under the whole heaven there has not been done the like of what has been done to Jerusalem**. Israel's **shame of face** and disgrace is total, and they have no one to blame but themselves. **Yahweh** their **God** is **righteous in all** His **works**.

> [15] And now, O Lord our God, who brought Your people out of the land of Egypt with a mighty hand, and made Yourself a name, as it is this day—we have sinned, we have done wickedly. [16] O Lord, according to all Your righteousness, please let Your anger and Your wrath be turned away from Your city Jerusalem, Your holy mountain; because for our sins and for the iniquities of our fathers, Jerusalem and Your people are a reproach to all those around us. [17] Now therefore, O our God, hear the prayer of Your servant and his supplications, and for Your sake cause Your face to shine on Your sanctuary, which is desolate. [18] O my God, incline Your ear and hear; open Your eyes and see our desolations, and the city which is called by Your Name; for we do not present our supplications before You because of our righteousness, but because of Your great mercies. [19] O Lord, hear! O Lord, forgive! O Lord, listen and act!

> Do not delay for Your own sake, my God, for Your city and Your
> people are called by Your Name."

This long prayer and confession of sin make plain that Israel has
learned its lesson from the calamity, and that God therefore will not
regret restoring them. Daniel, having confessed his nation's sin in
thorough and unflinching terms, turns to asking for pardon and restoration. God **brought** His **people out of the land of Egypt with
a mighty hand** once before and thereby **made** Himself **a name**, a
reputation among the nations, as the wonderworking God of Israel,
which persists until that very **day**. Since Daniel acknowledges that
Israel has **sinned** and **done wickedly**, will the Lord **please let** His
anger and wrath be turned away?

After all, Jerusalem is His own **city**, His **holy mountain**, the
place He claimed for His own and where He caused His Name to
dwell. God's people and His city are now a byword, a **reproach**, a
standing disgrace **to all around** them. May the Lord hearken to
this prayer and smile once again on the **sanctuary, which is desolate**! May the Lord not be deaf to them, nor blind to the state of
His city! May He bend down His **ear** to **hear** the cry for mercy, and
open His **eyes** to **see** Jerusalem's pitiful condition! Daniel asks this
not because of any **righteousness** Israel may imagine itself to have,
but solely because of God's **great mercies**. The prayer ends with
a staccato series of cries from the heart: **hear! forgive! listen! act!**
May there be no more **delay**. After all, the **city** and its **people** are
called by God's **Name**, and they all belong to Him.

> [20] Now while I was speaking, praying, and confessing my sin and
> the sin of my people Israel, and presenting my supplication before
> Yahweh my God for the holy mountain of my God, [21] while
> I was speaking in prayer, the man Gabriel, whom I had seen in the
> vision at the first, came to me in swift flight at about the time of

the evening offering. ²² And he informed me, and spoke with me, and said, "O Daniel, I have now come forth to give you skill in understanding. ²³ At the beginning of your supplications the word went forth, and I have come to tell you, for you are greatly beloved; therefore, consider the word, and understand the vision:

As God promised, "while they are still speaking, I will hear" (Is. 65:24), so Daniel received an immediate answer from God. **While he was speaking, praying, and confessing his sin and the sin of his people, presenting a supplication for the holy mountain of his God**, he received another angelic visitation. The **man Gabriel** (so called because the angel "had the appearance of a man"; Dan. 8:15) came to him **in swift flight**. Gabriel is portrayed as arriving after a hurried journey, as coming on an important mission, with not a moment to lose.

The arrival was **at about the time of the evening offering**, not because the evening offering was sacrificed in the temple at that time, but because had the temple been standing, it would have been. We see from this temporal description how deeply the heart of God's people was united to the temple—even when the temple did not exist (having been destroyed in the conflagration of 586 BC), the pious still told time by its rhythms.

Gabriel's urgent message is that he has come to **give** Daniel **skill in understanding**. Because Daniel is **greatly beloved** by God, God instantly dispatched Gabriel to give him insight **at the beginning of** his **supplications**. That is, as soon as Daniel began praying, **the word went forth** from God, and Gabriel began his **swift flight**. Now, when Daniel has not even finished his entreaties, Gabriel arrives with a message (a **word**, Heb. *dabar*) and a **vision** (i.e., a revelation—not something seen, as in chapters seven and eight, but a verbal message, seen with the eyes of the heart). Daniel has indeed read the Scriptures containing Jeremiah's message about the end of Jerusalem's suffering and its desolation, but he does not yet fully understand all its hidden significance. This is what Gabriel will now explain.

24 "Seventy weeks are decreed
    for your people and for your holy city,
    to finish the transgression,
    to make an end of sins,
    to atone for iniquity,
    to bring in everlasting righteousness,
    to seal up vision and prophecy,
    and to anoint the most holy place.
25 Know therefore and understand,
    that from the going forth of the word to restore and build
    Jerusalem
    until an anointed one, a prince, there shall be seven weeks.
    For sixty-two weeks it shall be built again,
    with plaza and the moat,
    but in troubled times.
26 And after sixty-two weeks an anointed one shall be cut off,
    with no judgment for him,
    and the people of the prince who is to come
    shall devastate the city and the sanctuary,
    and its end shall be with a flood,
    and till the end of the war desolations are decreed.
27 Then he shall confirm a covenant with many for one week,
    but in the middle of the week
    he shall cause sacrifice and offering to cease,
    and abomination of desolation shall be in its place,
    until the destruction which is decreed
    is poured out on the desolator."

The message is this: **seventy weeks are decreed** by God for Daniel's **people** and **for** his **holy city to finish the transgression, to make an end of sins, to atone for iniquity, to bring in everlasting righteousness, to seal up vision and prophecy, and to anoint the most holy place** (i.e., the temple). In his reading of the prophecy of Jeremiah, Daniel had concluded that at the end of seventy years the suffering of Israel and the desolation of the holy city would be over, and a period of peace, righteousness, and triumph would begin. Sadly, this would not be so.

The vision of the seventy weeks was not given to Daniel to contradict the prophecies of Jeremiah (as it might initially seem), but to further reveal its hidden meanings. Daniel supposed the prophecy meant that after seventy years Israel would turn the page and no longer suffer as the plaything of tyrants and the plunder of kings. He therefore prayed that God would fulfill His prophetic word and bring the promised prosperity, security, and peace. For the prophecy was clear: from the time Jeremiah spoke at the beginning of the exile, Israel would have to wait seventy years for the kingdom.

But the angel came with the revelation that there was a deeper way to understand these prophecies. The prophecies were not wrong, but they contained hidden and hitherto unsuspected depths and historical applications: the time of waiting would indeed last for seventy—but seventy *weeks* of years, not just years. From the time Jeremiah spoke and God sent forth His word that Jerusalem would be built, the time of waiting would be seventy sevens—490 years. As mentioned above, the common man had little access to precise historical records, and little concern for such exactitude anyway, so these numbers were used as much symbolically as historically. Before the promised peace could come, even more suffering awaited Israel in its long life after the exile.

We note here a continuation of the pattern seen in the transition throughout the Book of Daniel, and from chapter seven to chapter eight—namely, one of increasingly sharper focus and increasing concern for detail. Thus in chapter seven we saw only how the little horn thought to make changes in the times and in the law, speaking words against the Most High (7:25); in chapter eight we saw how this involved taking away the daily sacrifice 2300 times (8:11f). Here we focus further on this outrage and look to the restoration of the daily sacrifice and the doom of the one who removed it.

Daniel thought that after seventy years all would be well. He could not know of the future outrages of the little horn and the unprecedented suffering he would inflict on God's people, nor of the defilement of the temple he would commit. The promised **everlasting righteousness** for God's people and Jerusalem would indeed come, but not until much later than Daniel could imagine. Israel's preexilic **iniquity** would not take seventy *years* to be **atoned** for but seventy *weeks of years*. It was only after that time that their **transgression** would be **finished**, their **sins** be **made an end of**.

In the thought of the Old Testament, to forgive sin meant to bring peace and prosperity; to remember sin meant to bring disaster. Thus the widow of Zarephath concluded from the untimely death of her son that God had not forgiven her sin but still remembered it (1 Kin. 17:18). Thus the fact that Israel still suffered under Antiochus meant that Israel's sin had not been completely forgiven, but atonement and forgiveness were still to come. That atonement would come after seventy weeks. Then **vision and prophecy** would be **sealed** and authenticated through being fulfilled; then the temple's **most holy place** would be once and for all anointed.

Let Daniel **know therefore and understand** that a larger timeframe was involved when one truly understood Jeremiah's words. **From the going forth of the word to restore and build Jerusalem until an anointed one, a prince, there would be seven weeks**.

What was this **going forth of the word**? The use of the phrase in verse 23 to describe God's *dabar* sending Gabriel on his way indicates that it here describes not an earthly proclamation, but a divine word. One thinks of God's *dabar* through Jeremiah the prophet in verse 2.

God spoke through Jeremiah, saying that Jerusalem would be restored, and in the series of oracles found in Jeremiah 30—33, God indeed promised restoration: "Behold, days are coming when I will restore the fortunes of my people, Israel and Judah, and bring them back to the land . . . I will restore health to you . . . I will restore the fortunes of the tents of Jacob . . . the city shall be rebuilt upon its mound . . . behold, the days are coming when the city shall be rebuilt" (Jer. 30:3, 17, 18; 31:38). These oracles dated from about the time of the exile in 587 BC. Adding **seven weeks** or forty-nine years brings one to about 538, the time of the governor Zerubbabel, who with Joshua the high priest rebuilt the temple after the return from exile (Zech. 4:6f). In Zechariah 4:14, Zerubbabel along with Joshua is called an "anointed one" and so may justly be called an **anointed prince** (Heb. *meshiach nagid*).

After that time, **for sixty-two weeks**, Jerusalem shall **be built again, with plaza and moat**, and properly fortified. But this will be **in troubled times**—a reference no doubt to the efforts of Ezra and Nehemiah and all the difficulties that followed them throughout those years.

Then **after sixty-two weeks an anointed one shall be cut off**. This refers to the anointed priest Onias III, murdered in 171 BC. Onias was the high priest at the time of Antiochus Epiphanes but was forced to surrender the office to his brother Jason, who favored Antiochus's policy of Hellenization, which Onias strenuously opposed. His murder is recounted in 2 Maccabees 4. The period of sixty-two weeks or 434 years must be considered more symbolic than historically precise, and as a way of saying "toward the end of the seventy weeks." In this it resembles other ways of using numbers symbolically in apocalyptic literature.

In the *Book of Enoch*, in its "Apocalypse of Weeks," for example, we read that all human history consists of ten weeks, with the exile occurring in the sixth week and the Maccabean resistance occurring within the last three weeks. After that the age to come would arrive when there would be "many weeks without number forever" (*Enoch* ch. 93). Once again we see numbers used symbolically, without much regard for historical accuracy. The common man of that day had no resources to do the historical math. Saying the anointed one would be murdered after seven weeks and another sixty-two weeks of the seventy meant only "toward the final consummation."

The final description of the murder of the anointed one has vexed translators. Some render it, "shall be cut off having neither city nor sanctuary" (as a reference to Onias fleeing from Jerusalem to Daphne near Antioch for sanctuary); some render it as, "shall be cut off with no one to help him." The Greek Theodotion renders it as **with no judgment for him**—that is, without trial—and that is the rendering adopted here.

If the anointed "prince" (Heb. *nagid*) of verse 25 was indeed Zerubbabel the ruler, then **the prince** (Heb. *nagid*) **who is to come** in verse 26 would be the subsequent ruler in those days, Antiochus Epiphanes. His **people** did indeed **devastate the city and sanctuary** when he arrogantly entered the **sanctuary** and plundered it in 169 BC (1 Macc. 1:20–28) and later in 167 BC, when his men fell upon the city of Jerusalem, massacring many of its people and plundering the temple (1 Macc. 1:29–35). The **end** of the city came **with a flood**, as it suffered desolations until **the end of the war**—an accurate description of the ongoing warfare waged by the Maccabees.

We come finally to the dreadful heart of the catastrophe, which had been brought into increasingly sharper focus throughout the visions. We first saw how the little horn thought to "change the times and the law" (7:25), then how the sanctuary was overthrown and the daily sacrifice taken away (8:11). Now we learn how he **confirmed a covenant with many for one week** (i.e., seven years), but **in the middle of the week** (i.e., after three and a half years) he **caused sacrifice and offering to cease**.

The **covenant** here refers to Antiochus's alliances with the many renegade Hellenizing Jews in Israel. By dealing with the Syrian prince, the Hellenizers no doubt thought they were doing what was best for Israel—modernizing their faith, bringing it into the next century and the wider world. They could not know of the outrages to come when Antiochus found himself opposed and frustrated. But the unthinkable happened, and Antiochus set up the **abomination of desolation in its place** in the temple and forbade the offering of authentic Jewish sacrifice. This sacrifice would remain suspended for over three years, from 167–164 BC—poetically styled "time, times, and half a time" in 7:25 and here as "half a week."

What was this **abomination of desolation** of Antiochus (referred to also in 1 Macc. 1:54) that so defiled the altar? It is possible it was a pagan altar or an idol erected atop the Jewish one (1 Macc. 4:43 mentions the priests later removing the defiled stones to an unclean place), on which pagan altar swine were sacrificed (2 Macc. 6:4–5 mentions things brought to the altar that were unfit for sacrifice, abominable offerings forbidden by the Jewish laws). It is possible the mere presence of unclean offerings was what caused the temple stones to be regarded as defiled. Whatever the exact nature of the abomination of desolation (i.e., the sacrilege that makes desolate), it defiled the altar in the temple and made it unfit for sacrifice until it could be cleansed.

The final fate of the **desolator** is described in few words. He would prosper in his wretched work **until the destruction which is decreed is poured out on the desolator**. For all his might, his doom is assured, for it has been decreed by God. We note in this apocalypse that many things are described as decreed and set by the will of God—not only the seventy weeks of years (9:24) and the destructions of warfare (9:26), but the fate of all men, which lies in the hand of God as His watchers carry out the divine decrees regarding their rise and fall (4:17). God decides which empire will succeed another (hence the dreams and visions of chapters two, seven, and eight); God decides whether a tyrant shall prosper or perish.

THE VISION OF THE SEVENTY WEEKS CONTINUES THE pattern of escalating intensity noted earlier. The visions become not only more detailed but more overwhelming. In this story, after consulting the Scriptures, Daniel begins to pray for the restoration of Jerusalem and its temple. Before he even finishes praying, an angel comes rushing to him with the news that as soon as he began his prayer, God sent the angel on his way with a revelation for Daniel.

We have seen angels before in the Book of Daniel—an angel was sent to the three youths in the furnace, and an angel stayed with Daniel during his night in the lions' den. But here we find something more—a one-on-one conversation with an angel, who does not simply quench fire and shut the mouths of lions but gives a long message. As a child hearing the story would realize, the presence of the angel is almost as important as the message he brings, for all by itself the angel's presence reveals how important Daniel and God's people are, and how He listens intently to His people's prayers. God watches over His own, even when they are in faraway Babylon, deprived of the temple and the normal means of grace. The arrival of the angel, sent from God as soon as Daniel opened his mouth, showed the loving care of God for His faithful children.

One can imagine that the newer and deeper meaning of the prophecies the angel brought to Daniel must have filled him with some discouragement, for if Daniel thought Israel's sufferings in the world were almost over, it cannot have been welcome news that Israel would have to wait almost half a millennium before their sufferings would be finished. But the prophecy of the seventy weeks, received by those in Maccabean times, would have been much more encouraging, for the words meant that *for them* deliverance was at hand. The long-awaited everlasting righteousness (9:24) was about to come.

After such an exciting story, the listener or reader might think no more excitement was possible. What could top an angel rushing to one's side to bring such a detailed message when one was in prayerful mid-sentence? The final vision of the Book of Daniel brings the answer.

The Final Vision

10 [1] In the third year of Cyrus King of Persia,[44] a word was revealed to Daniel, whose name was called Belteshazzar. The word was true, and it was a great warfare, and he understood the word and had understanding of the vision. [2] In those days I, Daniel, was mourning three whole weeks. [3] I ate no pleasant food, no meat or wine came into my mouth, nor did I anoint myself at all, till three whole weeks were fulfilled. [4] Now on the twenty-fourth day of the first month, as I was by the bank of the great river, that is, the Tigris, [5] I lifted my eyes and looked, and behold!—a certain man clothed in linen, whose loins were girded with fine gold! [6] His body was like beryl, his face like the appearance of lightning, his eyes like fiery torches, his arms and feet like the gleam of burnished bronze, and the sound of his words like the sound of a multitude. [7] And I, Daniel, alone saw the vision, for the men who were with me did not see the vision; but a great trembling fell upon them, and they fled to hide themselves. [8] So I was left alone and saw this great vision, and no strength was left in me, for I turned deathly pale and retained no strength. [9] Then I heard the sound of his words, and when I heard the sound of his words I was lying stunned on my face, with my face to the ground. [10] And behold!—a hand touched me and set me shaking on my knees and on the palms of

---

44   The use of the title "king of Persia" is unhistorical to describe Cyrus after he conquered Babylon; after his victory he was described as "king of Babylon" or "the great king" or "king of the lands." Such a use of the title to describe him after his victory did not become common until Hellenistic times—another indication of the late date of the book.

my hands. [11] And he said to me, "O Daniel, greatly beloved man, understand the words that I speak to you and stand upright, for now I have been sent to you." While he was speaking this word to me, I stood trembling. [12] Then he said to me, "Fear not, Daniel, for from the first day that you set your heart to understand and humble yourself before your God, your words were heard, and I have come because of your words. [13] The ruler of the kingdom of Persia withstood me twenty-one days, and behold!—Michael, one of the chief rulers, came to help me, so I left him there with the kings of Persia. [14] Now I have come to make you understand what will happen to your people in the latter days, for the vision is for many days yet to come." [15] When he had spoken to me according to these words, I turned my face toward the ground and became speechless. [16] And behold!—one having the form of the sons of men touched my lips; then I opened my mouth and spoke, saying to him who stood before me, "My lord, because of the vision my pains have overwhelmed me, and I have no strength left. [17] For how can this servant of my lord speak with you, my lord? As for me, now no strength remains in me, nor is any breath left in me." [18] Then again, the one having the form of a man touched me and strengthened me. [19] And he said, "O man greatly beloved, fear not! Peace be with you; be strong, yes, be strong!" So when he spoke to me, I was strengthened and said, "Let my lord speak, for you have strengthened me." [20] Then he said, "Do you know why I have come to you? And now I will return to fight with the ruler of Persia; and when I have gone forth, then behold!—the ruler of Greece will come. [21] But I will tell you what is inscribed in the Writing of Truth. No one upholds me in these things except Michael your ruler. 11 [1] As for me, in the first year of Darius the Mede, I stood up to confirm and strengthen him."

As in 7:1 and 8:1, the narrator steps on stage only long enough to introduce Daniel, who once again narrates the vision in the first person for greater dramatic effect. It is dated to **the third year of Cyrus king of Persia**, so that the visions follow one another chronologically and the listener can track their building intensity. By hearing yet again that Daniel **was called Belteshazzar,** we are reminded of his long history at the Babylonian court and his long history of receiving revelations, and we are thus prepared for this final vision. The word or revelation was described as **true** and also as **a great warfare** (Heb. *sabah*, sometimes translated "army"), probably because it concerned extended warfare on earth and came as the fruit of extended angelic warfare in the heavenlies (vv. 13, 20–21). The narrator mentions twice in verse 1 that this time Daniel **understood the word and had understanding of the vision** (unlike previous visions; compare 7:28; 8:27)—doubtless because now the vision was given in such fine detail.

We are prepared for the increased intensity of the vision by the fact that Daniel says he **was mourning three whole weeks**, fasting entirely from **food, meat,** and **wine**—a considerably longer period than that of his former fast, mentioned in 9:3. Such was his fervency that he did not even **anoint** himself **at all**, rejecting such basic hygiene, as one does when in deep mourning (compare 2 Sam. 14:2). Fasting was a way of seeking God and preparing oneself to receive revelation, as we see from 2 Esdras 5:13; 6:35. The three weeks of fasting, terminating **the twenty-fourth of the first month**, mean that Daniel would have fasted through the Feasts of Passover and the Unleavened Bread, showing the urgency of his prayer.

His fasting was rewarded, for one day he **lifted** his **eyes** and suddenly saw **a certain man clothed in linen** (the dress of a priest), **whose loins were girded with fine gold.** Not only were his garments unusual, his form was astounding also, for **his body was like beryl** (compare the vision of the angelic chariots in Ezek. 1:16), **his**

face was like **lightning, his eyes like fiery torches, his arms and feet like the gleam of burnished bronze, and the sound of his words** like a roaring **multitude**.

Daniel alone saw the vision; his colleagues who were with him **did not see the vision** but **fled to hide themselves.** Their flight suggests the vision itself was preceded by a flash of light or by something that inspired terror in those who were with Daniel. Their flight and abandonment of Daniel emphasize how terrifying the vision is.

Daniel had seen angels in visions before (8:15f; 9:21), but none had affected him like this. Once before a vision had left him stunned to the ground (8:17–18), but this was altogether more frightening. **No strength was left** in him (emphasized twice in v. 8), and he turned **deathly pale** (some translations render this as "my vigor dissolved into confusion" and some as "I became utterly distraught"), **lying stunned on** his **face**. It was only gradually and with angelic help that he was at length able to come **shaking** to a position on his **hands** and **knees** and then to a **trembling** upright position.

The angel addresses Daniel as he did on a previous occasion, as **greatly beloved** (9:23), and therefore the chosen recipient of such a mighty revelation. Also just like the last time an angel visited him, Daniel is told that God responded immediately to his prayer. He had been praying for three weeks, and yet **from the first day that** he **set** his **heart to understand** what would happen to Israel, his **words were heard,** and the angel had now come because of his prayer.

Why then the delay in the angel's arrival? This was not due to any divine reluctance to answer (the angel was sent by God immediately), but was entirely due to warfare in the heavenlies: the unseen **ruler of the kingdom of Persia withstood** him for all the last **twenty-one days** and would not let him pass. Then suddenly

Michael, one of the chief rulers, came to help him with the conflict. He **left** Michael there to wage his warfare and continued on his way to meet Daniel and answer his prayer by making him **understand what will happen to** his **people in the latter days**, after **many days yet to come**.

Such extraordinary news of war in the heavenlies and of such a revelation prove too much for Daniel, and he again collapses, once again needing angelic assistance before he can even speak. The angel therefore **touched** his **lips** to restore their use so they could converse. The exchange between Daniel and the angel stressed both Daniel's weakness (mentioned again twice) and how he was strengthened by the angel (mentioned three times). The angel even exhorts Daniel repeatedly, saying, **"Peace be with you; be strong, yes, be strong!"**

These words are not simply filler or empty conversation. Rather, they express the main theme of the coming content, and one of the main themes in the entire Book of Daniel: God gives His people **peace** (i.e., safety), and He gives them strength. Through His help, Israel is made **strong**; safe in His care, they will survive and overcome all their foes. This is not through any merit or military genius of their own, but only because God sends His angels to fight for them. Michael, who has come to rescue and support this angel, will also support Israel to rescue them.

The angel then asked if Daniel knows **why** he **has come**, setting up the narrative for a dramatic answer. His answer (contained in chapters eleven to twelve) must be brief, for he was in a hurry **to return to fight with the ruler of Persia** and rejoin the battle in the heavenlies. After Persia was conquered, **the ruler of Greece** would **come** so that he must fight against him too. With such conflict awaiting him, there was no time to lose. He would therefore now recount quickly the future, things that were **inscribed in the**

Writing of Truth, the heavenly book containing God's will for the future. The warfare would be strenuous, for the angel had **no one** to **uphold** him **in these** battles **except Michael**, described (encouragingly for Israel) as **your ruler**. The angels supported each other as they carried out God's will. As Michael upheld him, so **in the first year of Darius the Mede**, when Babylon fell, he **stood up to confirm and strengthen him**.

The concept of angelic warfare in the heavenlies having a decisive effect upon earthly history is foreign to our culture and historical understanding, but it was widespread in the ancient world. Each nation had its guardian angel or its tutelary spirit, and these would defend their peoples below, warring with other spirits for supremacy. In paganism these forces were originally regarded as the gods of the various nations, but monotheistic Israel preferred to speak of angels and guardians, all under the ultimate sovereignty of God. Thus in 2 Maccabees 5:1–4 we find a description of "golden clad horsemen charging through the air, in companies fully armed with lances and drawn swords—troops of horsemen drawn up, attacks and counterattacks made on this side and that." It is true this was but a vision, an apparition, but it was a vision of something that was believed to occur in the unseen realms.

And not only in Israel were these things believed, but the Church too knows of warfare in the heavenlies, with the angels of God warring against the angels of the devil (Rev. 12:7–9), the demonic rulers and powers in the heavenly places (Eph. 6:12). The concepts presented here, like everything in the Scriptures, are not outdated mythology but divine truth.

In this passage we see clearly how the victories and defeats of the nations have their ultimate and unseen cause in the heavenly realms. Michael and Gabriel overthrew Babylon when **Darius the Mede** received the kingdom (5:30). Now it was Persia's turn. During this

third year of Cyrus King of Persia (10:1), the **kings of Persia** were vainly trying to withstand and to fight against Michael. After the Persian kingdom, the kingdom of Greece would come to oppose God and would be opposed by Michael too. History was full of one war after another, yet all lay ultimately in the hands of the God of the Jews. God had made the angel Michael strong enough to vanquish all, and it was he who was Israel's **ruler** and angelic protector.

> [2] "And now I will tell you the truth: Behold!—three more kings shall arise in Persia, and the fourth shall be far richer than all; when he is strong through his riches, he shall stir up all against the kingdom of Greece. [3] Then a mighty king shall arise, who shall rule with great dominion and do according to his will. [4] And when he has arisen, his kingdom shall be broken and divided toward the four winds of heaven, but not to his posterity, nor according to his dominion with which he ruled, for his kingdom shall be pulled up and given to others besides these.

The angel now proceeded to reveal the future as written in the divine Writing of Truth. The angel skipped quickly over the Persian and Greek periods to concentrate in minute detail upon what is evidently his real concern, the time of Antiochus Epiphanes. In the previous chapters, the kings of the world's empires appeared as symbols—as different metallic parts of a great statue, or as different monstrous beasts arising from a turbulent sea, or as many horns sprouting from the heads of those beasts. Now they appeared as they did in history, as men, kings, and soldiers. The perspective of the apocalyptic seer now gives place to the perspective of the common man and the historian. Here, we discover at last, is what those metals, beasts, and horns really look like. No wonder that Daniel said he "understood the word" (10:1).

The Persian and Greek Empires

The interpreting angel began by narrating the future history of Persia and by revealing that **three more kings shall arise in Persia, and the fourth shall be far richer than all** of them and **shall stir up all against the kingdom of Greece**.[45] After the Persians, **a mighty king shall arise, who shall rule with great dominion and do** whatever he wants, conquering whom he will. This was Alexander the Great, who defeated the Persian Darius III in 330 BC, thereby becoming master of the Persian Empire and founder of the Macedonian or Greek one.

Soon afterward, however, Alexander died an early and untimely death by disease in 323 BC, and **his kingdom** was **divided toward the four winds of heaven**. Ultimately, however, it was **not** inherited by **his posterity** or his children but was **given to others besides these**, to his generals. After a short time, four centers of power became prominent: Macedonia and Greece; Thrace and Asia Minor; northern Syria, Babylonia, and the East; and Egypt. The ones that affected those living in the Holy Land were the rulers of Egypt and Syria. Palestine was included in the orbit of Egypt.

The Kingdoms of the Egyptian Ptolemies and the Syrian Seleucids

After this quick and cursory recitation of the Persian and Macedonian or Greek empires, the narrative comes to the contest that mostly affected Israel, that between the Egyptian part of Alexander's empire in the south ("the king of the South") and the Syrian or

---

45   If the narrative is meant as a full history, this is another historical error, for after Cyrus there were not just three or four kings in Persia, but thirteen in total from Cyrus to the last one, Darius III. The one who was richer than all, Xerxes (his wealth is mentioned by Herodotus), was indeed the fourth king after Cyrus. The one who went to war against the Greeks and was defeated by Alexander was not Xerxes but Darius III, who lived over a hundred years later.

Seleucid part of his empire in the north ("the king of the North"). The contrast between the historical generalities of chapters one to ten and chapter eleven is very stark. Here we find a fine and detailed knowledge of political events utterly unlike the history recounted in earlier chapters, a knowledge which suggests that the events occurred recently.

> [5] Then the king of the South shall be strong, and one of his rulers shall be stronger than he, and his dominion shall be a great dominion.

Verse 5, Ptolemy I Soter and Seleucus I

The **king of the South** in verse 5 is Ptolemy I Soter (323–285 BC), who ruled Egypt after the death of Alexander. **One of his** generals or **rulers** was Seleucus I Nicator, who recovered Babylonia, northern Syria, and other area besides. He thus became **stronger** than his former master Ptolemy and had **a great dominion**, ruling over a larger area once he had consolidated his power after 301 BC.

> [6] After some years they shall join together, and the daughter of the king of the South shall go to the king of the North to make an alliance; but she shall not keep the strength of her arm, and his offspring will not endure; but she shall be given up, with those who brought her, and with him who fathered her and supported her.

Verse 6, Ptolemy II and Antiochus II

After some years, in 250 BC, **king of the South** Ptolemy II Philadelphus (285–246) **joined together** with his rival Antiochus II Theos (261–246), the **king of the North**, by attempting a marriage alliance with his **daughter** Berenice. It did not go well: Antiochus divorced his wife Laodice to marry Berenice, then divorced her (**she shall be given up**) and returned to his wife. The matter ended with

Antiochus, Berenice, and their infant child all eventually being killed, and her father Ptolemy, who **fathered and supported her,** dying that year as well.

> In those times [7] a branch of her roots shall arise in its place, who shall come with an army, enter the fortress of the king of the North, and deal with them and prevail. [8] And he shall also carry off their gods, with their molten images and their precious vessels of silver and gold, captive to Egypt, and for some years he shall keep away from the king of the North. [9] Then the king of the North shall come to the kingdom of the king of the South, but shall return to his own land.

Verses 7–9, the revenge of Ptolemy III and defeat of Seleucus II

Then **a branch** of Berenice's **roots**, her brother Ptolemy III Euergetes, now on the throne of Egypt, **arose in** her **place** and worked to avenge her death. He **came with an army** and invaded the territory of Seleucus II Callinicus, conquering Seleucia and Antioch and putting to death Laodice, who had ordered the poisoning of his sister. He then returned to Egypt with much plunder, including **their precious vessels of silver and gold**. Later on Seleucus would recover some of his power and invade Egypt in 242. He could not prevail, however, and was forced to **return to his own land**.

> [10] And his sons shall wage war and assemble a multitude of great forces; and one shall come on and overflow and pass through, and will again carry the war as far as his fortress. [11] And the king of the South shall be enraged and go out and fight with him, with the king of the North, who shall raise a great multitude; but the multitude shall be given into his hand. [12] When he has carried away the multitude, his heart will be lifted up, and he will cast down tens of thousands, but he shall not prevail. [13] For the king of the

North will return and raise a multitude greater than the former, and after some years he shall come with a great army and abundant supplies. ¹⁴ Now in those times many shall rise up against the king of the South, and men of violence among your people shall exalt themselves in order to establish the vision, but they shall stumble. ¹⁵ Then the king of the North shall come and throw up siege-works, and take a fortified city, and the forces of the South shall not stand. Even his picked troops shall have no strength to resist. ¹⁶ But he who comes against him shall do according to his own will, and no one shall stand before him. He shall stand in the Beautiful Land with destruction in his power. ¹⁷ He shall also set his face to come with the strength of his whole kingdom and make an agreement with him; thus shall he do. And he shall give him the daughter of women to destroy him; but it shall not stand with him or be for him. ¹⁸ After this he shall turn his face to the coastlands and shall take many. But a commander shall put an end to his insolence to wear him out, and shall turn his insolence back on him. ¹⁹ Then he shall turn his face toward the fortresses of his own land, but he shall stumble and fall, and not be found.

Verses 10–19, Antiochus III

The **sons** of the king of the North, Seleucus II, in verse 10 were Seleucus III Keraunus (226–223), who ruled briefly before being murdered, and Antiochus III the Great (226–187), who succeeded him. They **waged war** with a **multitude of great forces**. Antiochus invaded, reaching the **fortress** itself (possibly Raphia near the Egyptian border). The king of the South, Ptolemy IV Philopater (221–203), was **enraged** and defeated the **great multitude** raised by Antiochus with great slaughter in 217. Despite his victory, Ptolemy did **not prevail** or gain territory. The king of Egypt, moral degenerate that he was, did not press his advantage but was content simply to make peace with Antiochus.

After fourteen years, Antiochus's power had grown, and he was ready to press his claims on Egypt. Ptolemy IV had died and been replaced by his young son, Ptolemy V Epiphanes (203–181). Antiochus invaded the south, along with **many** who wanted to shake free of the Egyptian power. Some **men of violence** in Palestine **exalted** themselves to fight against Antiochus, but they **stumbled** and failed. Antiochus **threw up siege-works** and took the **fortified city** of Sidon in 198, despite the Egyptian general Scopas's use of his **picked troops**. With this victory, Antiochus the Great won possession of all Palestine, which passed under Seleucid rule. The **Beautiful Land** of God's people lay **in his power**.

Antiochus, however, did not dare to invade Egypt. Instead he gave to young Egyptian Ptolemy V his daughter Cleopatra, the **daughter of women,** in marriage. Antiochus hoped therefore to **destroy** Ptolemy, but his plan did **not stand or be** a success **for him**. Instead Cleopatra proved loyal to her husband and to Egypt. Frustrated at this, Antiochus **turned his face to the coastlands** of Greece, despite the warnings of Rome to stay away. Here he was beaten by the Roman **commander** Scipio at Magnesia in 190, so that **his insolence** was **turned back on him**. Humiliated, he returned **to the fortresses of his own land** of Syria, Mesopotamia, and the East. When he tried to pillage a local temple of Bel in Elymais to pay his debts to Rome, he **stumbled and fell**—he was assassinated by the local people.

> [20] There shall arise in his place one who imposes taxes for the glory of the kingdom, but within a few days he shall be broken, but not in anger or in battle.

Verse 20, Seleucus IV Philopator

Antiochus III was succeeded on his throne by his son Seleucus IV (187–175). In 2 Maccabees 3, we read the story of his failed attempt to plunder the temple at Jerusalem through his tax collector, Heliodorus. The description of him as **one who imposes taxes for the glory of the kingdom** refers to this incident. He died after a comparatively brief reign of twelve years, but **not in** the **anger** of a brawl **or in** the heat of **battle**, as might befit a conquering king. Rather he was assassinated in a plot planned by his tax collector.

The Tyrannous Reign of Antiochus IV Epiphanes

The recitation of the history of the Persians and Greeks gives way to a lengthier recitation of the history of the conflicts between the Ptolemies and the Seleucids, but this mostly serves as introduction to the real central topic of the final vision—the tyranny and persecution of Antiochus Epiphanes. Accordingly, his reign is recounted in the most detail of all.

> ²¹ And in his place shall arise a contemptible person to whom royal majesty has not been given; he shall come in peaceably and seize the kingdom by deceit.

Verse 21, Assumption of Power

He is first described as one **to whom royal majesty has not been given**. The original heir to the throne was the son of Seleucus IV, Demetrius. Antiochus had been living luxuriously in Rome as a hostage, and he was exchanged there for Demetrius, his nephew. The throne was seized by Heliodorus, under the pretext that he was acting as regent for another Antiochus, the younger son of Seleucus. Heliodorus fled when Antiochus IV raised an army and seized the throne, supposedly on behalf of Demetrius in Rome, along with the other Antiochus as coregent. This coregent was murdered in 170, so that Antiochus was said to **seize the kingdom by deceit**.

> ²² Armies shall be swept away from before him and be broken, and the prince of the covenant also. ²³ And after a covenant is made with him, he shall act deceitfully, for he shall come up and become strong with a few people. ²⁴ He shall enter peaceably, even into the richest places of the province, and he shall do what his fathers have not done, nor his fathers' fathers—he shall distribute among them plunder, spoil, and riches, and he shall devise his plans against strongholds, but only for a time. ²⁵ He shall stir up his power and his courage against the king of the South with a great army. And the king of the South shall wage war with a very great and mighty army, but he shall not stand, for plots shall be devised against him. ²⁶ Even those who eat of his rich food shall break him, and his army shall be swept away, and many shall fall down slain. ²⁷ Both these kings' hearts shall be bent on evil, and they shall speak lies at the same table; but it shall not prosper, for the end will still come at the appointed time. ²⁸ While returning to his land with great riches, his heart shall be set against the holy covenant, and he shall act and return to his own land.

Verses 22–28, First War with Egypt

Antiochus continued to prosper as **armies** were **swept away from before him** and their power was **broken**, including that of **the prince of the covenant**, the Jewish high priest Onias III, who effectively ruled the country. Onias resisted Antiochus's program of Hellenization and so was replaced by his more pliable brother, Jason (who himself was soon replaced by even more Hellenizing Menelaus). Antiochus thus **made a covenant** with the rulers of Judea, promising them peace. He gathered up wealth from the **richest places of the province**, **distributing among them plunder, spoil, and riches** to secure their loyalty and consolidate his power as he **devised** further **plans**.

Antiochus then undertook his first campaign against Egypt, **the king of the South,** in 169. The king of the South was the young King Ptolemy VI Philometer, who received bad advice from his Egyptian advisors who **ate of his rich food**, for they urged him to attack Syria and Palestine and recover them for Egypt. Antiochus met the invaders, who could **not stand** before him. Antiochus crushed their army at the frontier city of Pelusium in 169. Ptolemy followed more bad advice and fled but was caught and taken captive by Antiochus.

Ptolemy and Antiochus then sat down to negotiate (**speak lies**) **at the same table**, ostensibly to join forces against Philometer's brother, newly crowned as Ptolemy VII. Each **king's heart was bent on evil** and advancing his own agenda, but they did **not prosper**, for the two Ptolemies later united against Antiochus. Unable to control Egypt, he **returned to his** own **land with great** plundered **riches**. Frustrated at his failure, he **set his heart against the holy covenant**, for he heard that the former high priest Jason had many supporters of his rival Menelaus murdered. Antiochus **acted** swiftly and massacred many Jews, reinstated Menelaus, looted the temple, and then **returned to his land**.

> [29] At the appointed time he shall return and come into the south, but this time shall not be as before. [30] For ships of Cyprus shall come against him, and he shall be grieved, and return in rage against the holy covenant, and act. So he shall return and show regard for those who forsake the holy covenant.

Verses 29–30, Second War with Egypt

At hearing the news that the reconciled Ptolemies were planning to join forces against Syria, Antiochus **returned and came into the south**, again invading Egypt in 168. **But this time** he would not be successful: **ships of Cyprus** carrying a Roman delegation gave him the order to desist from threatening Alexandria and to leave Egypt, and Antiochus had no choice but to comply. Furious at his humiliation, he **returned in rage**, determined to tighten his grip on Palestine and enforce his authority there against all resisters who still clung to the ancestral ways of **the holy covenant**. In this he had the cooperation of the Hellenizing party of the Jews, here called **those who forsake the holy covenant**.

> [31] And forces from him shall appear, and they shall desecrate the sanctuary fortress; then they shall take away the daily sacrifice and set up the abomination of desolation. [32] Those who do wickedly against the covenant he shall corrupt through flattery; but the people who know their God shall be strong and take action. [33] And those of the people who understand shall instruct many, yet for many days they shall fall by sword and flame, by captivity and plunder. [34] When they stumble, they shall be helped with a little help, but many shall join with them in hypocrisy. [35] And some of those of understanding shall stumble, to refine them, purify, and whiten, until the time of the end, because it is yet for the appointed time. [36] And the king shall act according to his own will; he shall magnify and exalt himself above every god, shall speak awesome things against the God of gods, and shall prosper till the wrath has been accomplished, for what has been decreed shall be done. [37] He shall regard neither the god of his fathers nor the one women love, nor regard any god, for he shall exalt himself above them all. [38] But in his place he shall honor a god of fortresses, and a god which his fathers did not know he shall honor with gold and silver, with precious stones and costly things. [39] And he shall act against

the strongest fortresses with the aid of a foreign god. Those who acknowledge him he shall advance with glory, and he shall make them to rule over many, and divide the land for gain.

Verses 31–39, Blasphemous Tyranny in Palestine

Those who resisted Antiochus's policy of Hellenization fomented revolt, which was dealt with severely. The king sent Apollonius, commander of his mercenaries, to massacre a number of them and to plunder and destroy the city of Jerusalem. These soldiers, **forces from him, desecrated the sanctuary fortress** by garrisoning pagan soldiers there. The rites of Judaism were banned, the **daily sacrifice** (Heb. *tamid*) was taken away, and the pagan sacrificial altar, **the abomination of desolation**, was **set up**, in 167 BC.

Palestine was divided. Some Jews **did wickedly against the covenant** (i.e., favored the king's policies), and these Antiochus **corrupted through flattery**, offering them his customary lavish gifts and bribes. Other Jews who **knew their God** (i.e., who resisted the royal policy of Hellenization) were **strong** and **took action**. Certain of them could **understand** the significance of the times and took care to **instruct many**, teaching them to resist the inducements to apostasy. But King Antiochus worked to root them out, and **for many days** they **fell by sword and flame, by captivity and plunder**.

These men were the pious ones (Heb. *Hasidim*), those who clung to their ancestral faithfulness and for whom devotion to God was paramount. When they **stumbled** and fell to Antiochus, they were **helped with a little help**—the resistance of the Maccabees and their paramilitary opposition to the king. **Many joined** the cause of the Hasidim, but **in hypocrisy**, supporting the armed Maccabees while caring for God only superficially in their hearts. These times were a crucible, testing what lay in the hearts of men. **Some** of the pious fell through persecution, as God's providence came to **refine, purify, and whiten** Israel in preparation for the **appointed** consummation at **the time of the end**.

Those were terrible days. The king **acted according to his own will**, unhampered by any, and **magnified and exalted himself above every god**. In his coins he styled himself not just "King Antiochus" (as earlier) but now "King Antiochus, God Manifest, Victory-bringer." He also blasphemed **the God of gods**, outlawing Jewish worship. He was allowed by God to **prosper till the wrath** against Israel was **accomplished**, for this also had been **decreed** by God.

Even by pagan standards, Antiochus acted improperly in his pride. He impiously abandoned the **god of his fathers** (the Seleucids seem to have worshipped Apollo as their patron) as well as the deity **women love**, probably Adonis/Tammuz (compare Ezek. 8:14). Instead, with cynical pragmatism he **honored a god of fortresses**—probably a reference to the introduction of pagan cults by his troops garrisoned in the fortresses of Judea, possibly that of Zeus Olympius as their supreme patron, a custom **his fathers did not know**. Thus he acted against the **strongest fortresses** of Judea with **the aid of** the **foreign god** worshipped by his soldiers garrisoned there. These habits revealed the impiety of Antiochus, who in reality cared for the honor neither of gods nor of men. He would **advance with glory** any who **acknowledged him**, lavishing on them both power to **rule over many** and **land for gain**.

> [40] At the time of the end, the king of the South shall attack him,
> and the king of the North shall come against him like a storm,
> with chariots, horsemen, and with many ships; and he shall come
> into countries, and overflow, and pass through. [41] He shall also
> enter the Beautiful Land, and tens of thousands shall stumble,
> but these shall escape from his hand: Edom, Moab, and the chiefs
> of the sons of Ammon. [42] He shall stretch out his hand against

the countries, and the land of Egypt shall not escape. [43] He shall rule over the treasures of gold and silver, and over all the precious things of Egypt; also the Libyans and Ethiopians shall follow at his heels. [44] Then reports from the east and the north shall alarm him; therefore, he shall go out with great fury to devastate and annihilate many. [45] And he shall plant his royal tents between the seas and the glorious holy mountain; yet he shall come to his end, and no one will help him."

Verses 40–45, Antiochus's final end

At this point in the narrative, we make the transition from history to hope, from the verified record to the poetry of the prophetic. All the preceding parts of the vision were historically accurate, down to the fine details. The final career and the end of Antiochus, however, bear no relation whatever to the historical record. For after the persecution of the pious in Palestine, Antiochus went to Persia, where he attempted to plunder a temple in Elymais (compare 1 Macc. 6:1–17). Unsuccessful in his attempt, he withdrew to Tabae in Persia, became sick, and died there, in 164 BC. It appears as if these verses were written after his outrages in Palestine but before his departure to and death in Persia.

In this scenario, the Egyptian **king of the South** again **attacks him,** and he responds by counterattacking **like a storm**, passing through the **Beautiful Land** of Palestine again on the way. **Tens of thousands shall stumble** and fall before him, but not the countries of Edom, Moab, and the chiefs of Ammon, for his route keeps to the west of the Jordan. The **land of Egypt will not escape**, and he will plunder their **treasures of gold and silver**. The **Libyans** (bordering Egypt to the west) **and Ethiopians** (bordering it on the south) will **follow at his heels**—Egypt will be completely subdued.

When in Egypt, he will hear **reports** that will cause him to return toward **the east and the north**, eastward toward Persia and northward toward Armenia. Furious at this, he will once again **devastate and annihilate many** pious Jews in Palestine on the way. In that land he will **plant his royal tents between the seas and the glorious holy mountain** (i.e., between the Mediterranean and Mount Zion). Though he plot even more evil, he **shall come to his end**. God will strike him down in His own land, and **no one will help him**.

12

¹At that time Michael shall stand up,
the great ruler who keeps watch over the sons of your people,
and there shall be a time of trouble,
such as never was since there was a nation,
till that time.
And at that time your people shall be delivered,
every one who is found written in the Book.
²And many of those who sleep in the dust of the earth shall awake,
some to everlasting life,
some to shame and everlasting contempt.
³Those who are wise shall shine
like the brightness of the firmament,
and those who turn many to righteousness
like the stars forever and ever.

Verses 12:1–4, the Consummation

As with the destruction of the little horn in 7:26–27 (which signaled the beginning of the time when "the kingdom and the dominion shall be given to the people of the saints of the Most High"), and the destruction of the four empires of Nebuchadnezzar's image in 2:34–35 (which signaled the time when God's stone would "become a great mountain and fill the whole earth"), so the death of Antiochus signals the end of the age. After this final conflict, this age reaches its consummation. In the final conflagration, when Antiochus will devastate and annihilate many (11:44), **Michael, the great ruler who keeps watch** over Israel as their guardian angel, will **stand up** to fight for them and press their cause.

With these words, we return once more to the beginning of the vision, leaving the earthly historical events and ascending to the heavenly conflict unseen by men. In 10:20 we saw how the rise and fall of earthly kingdoms represented the outworking of angelic conflict in the heavenlies, and the political ascendancies of Persia and Greece were the result of the fighting of angels. Cyrus and Alexander might play their parts, but the day always belonged to the God of Israel. So it is here: the earthly fate and triumph of God's people would come through the heavenly exploits of Michael their ruler—and that triumph was at hand.

But the way to victory lay through conflict, **a time of trouble such as never was since there was a nation.** No one in Israel should imagine that their courage, perseverance, and blood would play no part in the coming triumph. The **time of trouble** would need all the heroism they could muster. The vision therefore ends not on a note of easy comfort, like a calming sedative, but on a note of rousing exultation, like a stirring battle cry. Let no one doubt the final outcome—God's **people** will be **delivered** and come at last to safety and receive the kingdom. These have their names **written in the Book** of God's favorite ones, His faithful (see Ex. 32:32–33; Is. 4:3; Mal. 3:16). And their heroism, perseverance, faithfulness, and martyrdom will have their full reward, as will acts of cowardice and apostasy: **many of those who sleep in the dust of the earth shall awake, some to everlasting life** and **some to shame and everlasting contempt.**

It is easy to read back into these words a fully developed and later Christian doctrine of the resurrection of all the dead, folding these words into those of John 5:28–29; 11:24; and Revelation 20:11–15.

This would be to ignore the fact that the truth unfolded gradually throughout the years in the Scriptures. Our text here does not assert the resurrection of all the dead. Its focus is solely on the just retribution of all those in the final time of trouble. Those who fail and betray their God **shall awake** to punishment, **to shame and everlasting contempt**, along with the persecutors of God's people. But those who remain faithful and persevere to the end **shall awake to everlasting life**. And **the wise**, those who not only persevere but also persuade **many** others to do so, **turning** them from potential apostasy to **righteousness**, shall **shine like the brightness of the firmament, like the stars forever and ever**.

The vision does not expound much on this final state of the bliss of the faithful, saying only that after the sleep of death they **awake** forever to **eternal life**. A bodily resurrection is clearly presupposed, but the nature of that resurrection and the answers to questions regarding what our bodies will be like then are not given. For that we must wait until the Second Coming of Christ (e.g., Matt. 22:30; 1 Cor. 15:35f). But we may be sure that what is promised as a reward for so harrowing a struggle will be great, and glorious, and worth the price. The **brightness of the firmament** with its burning **stars** promises a splendor beyond all imagining. It has not entered into the heart of man what God has prepared for those who love Him and who remain faithful to the death.

Final Angelic Command

⁴ "But you, Daniel, shut up the words, and seal the book until the time of the end; many shall run to and fro, and evil shall increase."

The vision that began in chapter ten with an overwhelming angelic epiphany and continued with a long recitation of future events from the Writing of Truth (10:21) now concludes with a final angelic command. Daniel must not reveal the contents of the words he has heard. They were not for his generation, but for the generation that would live to face the challenge from the little horn, the contemptible king of the North, Antiochus Epiphanes—that is, in the second century BC, at **the time of the end**. Accordingly Daniel must **shut up the words and seal the book** until then. When the final conflict came, then men could bring out the book and reveal its predictive contents. Then men could learn that all was foretold centuries before, and all lay in the hands of God, the One who directed the course of nations and held Israel's destiny.

What could be expected until that time? **Many** would **run to and fro**, looking in vain for a word from God (see Amos 8:12), and **evil**[46] would be **increased**. Times of spiritual famine and perplexity could be expected, times when evil would tempt and challenge the children of men. Let all take care therefore until the time of the consummation.

---

46   Thus the Old Greek of the original Septuagint, *adikias*. The Hebrew reading of the text as "knowledge" rather than "evil" is the result of reading the Hebrew *hara'ah* as *hadda'at*.

Epilogue

Daniel Goes His Way

⁵ Then I, Daniel, looked, and behold!—two others were standing, one on this riverbank and the other on that riverbank. ⁶ And one said to the man clothed in linen, who was above the waters of the river, "How long till the end of these awesome things?" ⁷ Then I heard the man clothed in linen, who was above the waters of the river, and he held up his right hand and his left hand toward heaven and swore by Him who lives forever that it shall be for a time, times, and half a time; and when they finish shattering the power of the holy people, all these things shall be finished. ⁸ And I heard, but I did not understand. Then I said, "My lord, what shall be the end of these things?" ⁹ And he said, "Go your way, Daniel, for the words are closed up and sealed till the time of the end. ¹⁰ Many shall be purified, whitened, and refined, but the wicked shall do wickedly, and none of the wicked shall understand, but the wise shall understand. ¹¹ And from the time the daily sacrifice is taken away, and the abomination of desolation is set up, there shall be one thousand two hundred and ninety days. ¹² Blessed is he who waits and comes to the one thousand three hundred and thirty-five days! ¹³ But as for you, go your way till the end; and you shall rest and will stand in your allotment at the end of the days."

The Book of Daniel concludes its message with a final exchange between Daniel and the angels. These were not the angelic rulers mentioned in chapter ten, but **two others**, standing suddenly (the suddenness is signaled by the usual **behold!**) near the **riverbank**, doubtless that of the Tigris, as at the beginning of the vision in 10:4. One of the angels appeared in human form, **clothed in linen** like a priest (as in 10:5). As in 8:13–14, where two angels had an exchange for the purpose of informing Daniel, so here the two angels exchange question and answer. The angel who was **above the waters** asked his fellow, "**How long till the end of these awesome things?**" The root of the word rendered here **awesome things** is connected to the word used in 11:36 to describe Antiochus's blasphemies, so that the question is, "When will Israel's long suffering come to an end and eternal righteousness be brought in?"

In response, the other angel **held up** not only **his right hand toward heaven** to **swear** an oath to God **who lives forever** (the normal way of taking an oath; see Deut. 32:40), but **his left hand** as well, making the oath doubly binding and his assurance doubly sure. He swore it would be for **a time, times, and half a time** (the three and a half years mentioned in 7:25), and when this defeat for Israel was **finished** and over, then these wonders would be **finished** as well. That is, the end of the persecution inflicted by the little horn, Antiochus Epiphanes, would mark the end of Israel's suffering. As in 7:25, the phrase does not represent a precise tally of days but indicates a time when the suffering is long, and then lengthened even more, and then suddenly cut short. Daniel's confession that he **heard** but **did not understand** increases the sense of mystery of the whole vision. The answer in itself was clear enough, but the staggering import of the revelation proved overwhelming to heart and understanding.

Daniel then asks another question, his last word in the book that bears his name. Bowing before the immensity of the visions he has received and properly respectful of the ones who brought it, he calls the angel **my lord** (a term of respect). Daniel himself was a great man, both in the world and before God, and the humble approach of such a great man to the bringer of the visions reveals how powerful these visions were. Reeling from a kind of spiritual vertigo, Daniel asks, "**What shall be the end of these things?**" To where does it all lead? What will happen after all this is fulfilled?

The final word belongs to the angel and to heaven, not to Daniel, and the angel does not answer Daniel's question. There will be no further revelation, no disclosure of what will happen after many awake from the dust of death to eternal life. Some realities are too wonderful for mere words, even words contained in visions or brought by angels. As C. S. Lewis wrote regarding such realities, "They were so great and beautiful that I cannot write them."

Instead, Daniel is bidden to **go** his **way** and live the rest of his life. The **words** he was given by the angel (and by extension, all his visions and revelations) were **closed up and sealed till the time of the end**. When the events of that end time occur and the meaning of the sealed words is revealed, then all Daniel's questions will be answered—but not until then.

This final time will be a time of testing, when **many shall be purified, whitened, and refined** by suffering (compare 11:35). It will also be a time of division, separating **the wicked** from **the wise**, the chaff from the wheat. **The wicked shall do wickedly**, so that none should be surprised at their apostasy. **The wicked** may offer convincing justifications for their actions, but let no one be deceived enough to join them: in their rejection of their ancestral faith, they **do wickedly**. That is because **none** of them **understand** the times in which they live or the significance of secularism. **The wise**, however, **shall understand** the true issues involved and will remain true to God.

Then the angels give a final chronological word: **from the time the daily sacrifice** (Heb. *tamid*) **is taken away and the abomination of desolation is set up** by Antiochus (8:11; 11:31) **shall be one thousand two hundred and ninety days. Blessed is he who waits and comes to the one thousand three hundred and thirty-five days!** It is safe to say that these figures have vexed commentators throughout the centuries. Given the difficulty of any second-century writer recovering all the copies of a book he had written and published, it seems unlikely that these represent two subsequent corrections to the original text of "time, times, and half a time" given in verse 7, as is sometimes suggested. It seems to refer to events following the persecution of God's people.

Some have suggested the figures represent dates for the death of Antiochus and for the time when news of his death was received in Palestine. Certainty is impossible, but it seems more likely that, like the expression "time, times, and half a time," these figures are used poetically to express ideas, rather than to date something with mathematical precision on a calendar. If the angel declined in verse 9 to give Daniel further details of what would occur afterward, it is unlikely he would then acquiesce to Daniel's request and indeed give more information in verses 11–12. The angel therefore is not referring here to specific events that will occur after 1290 days and 1335 days have elapsed. Rather, he is offering assurance that the time to come will be worth enduring the persecution. Let no one lose heart—a mere 1290 days after the outrage occurs, all will be well. A mere month and a half after that, such things will happen that anyone living to see them will declare himself **blessed** indeed. Attention should fall not so much on the numbers involved as on the verb **wait**. We now hope for what we do not see; let us wait for it with perseverance (Rom. 8:25).

The last word to Daniel is again an invitation to **go** his **way till**

the end of this life. Let him expect no more dreams or visions, no more angelic visitations. He was by now an old man; soon enough he would go the way of all flesh and rest in his grave. But his reward was sure, for he **will stand in** his **allotment at the end of the days**, inheriting his portion of the resurrection of the dead. He had proven himself wise in the midst of Babylon. He too would shine like the brightness of the firmament, like the stars forever and ever.

PART IV

Additions and Conclusion

ADDITIONS TO THE BOOK OF DANIEL

The Story of Susanna and the Story of Bel and the Serpent

In the Greek versions of the Book of Daniel, we find the *Story of Susanna* and the *Story of Bel and the Serpent* appended to the main text. Thus the Greek versions open not with a recitation of how exiles were taken from Judah to Babylon (Dan. 1:1f), but with the story of a man living in Babylon whose name was Jehoiakim, who had a wife named Susanna. In this story, the whole plight of the virtuous woman Susanna is recounted at length before, in answer to her desperate prayer, "God aroused the holy spirit of a young boy, whose name was Daniel" (who seems to have had no apparent connection with the Babylonian court at that time). In Daniel 1:6, however, Daniel and his friends are clearly being introduced for the first time, which makes no sense if he had in fact been introduced earlier, in the story of Susanna. For this reason it is evident that the story of Susanna was circulating separately before someone appended it to the Book of Daniel.

The *Story of Bel and the Serpent* also enjoyed an independent literary life before being appended to the end of the Book of Daniel. The Book of Daniel ends with 12:13, where Daniel is instructed by the angel to go his way to his rest and to wait for his final reward at the time of the end. Daniel is here dismissed from the literary stage as the book ends. This ill accords with the opening of *Bel and the Serpent*, which continues the adventures of Daniel.

Also, the stories exhibit neither of the two main themes of the Book of Daniel, which are (1) the necessity of maintaining integrity when under threat in a foreign land, and (2) the madness of pagan royal pride. These themes are consistently found in the adventure stories. Illustrating the theme of the necessity of maintaining integrity despite the threat of terrible consequences, we read of Daniel and his friends refusing the diet of the king in chapter one; Daniel's friends refusing to worship the giant image in chapter three; and Daniel refusing to cease praying to God in chapter six. Illustrating the theme of the madness of pagan royal pride, we read of Nebuchadnezzar's rage being countered and resolved by the supernatural revelation given to Daniel in chapter two; Nebuchadnezzar's pride being judged by God despite Daniel's supernatural revelation and warning in chapter three; and Belshazzar's blasphemy being judged by God as supernaturally revealed by Daniel in chapter five.

We see neither of these two main themes in the tale of Susanna or in the two tales of Bel and the serpent. There Daniel solves mysteries through non-supernatural means. He does not rely on revelations from God but simply uses a process of deduction and clever stratagem. Thus he vindicates Susanna's innocence by cross-examining the two false witnesses separately; he spreads ashes on the floor in Bel's temple to reveal the footprints of the priests and their families; and he makes a poisonous food for the serpent to eat unsuspectingly, causing it to die, thus proving that it is not divine. In all these tales he appears more like a detective than a man of supernatural visions. These stories do not fit the pattern of any of the other stories in the Book of Daniel but breathe an entirely different spirit.

Further, we find that the structure of the Book of Daniel is carefully crafted with the eye for balance of an artist. Consider the following structural elements in the Book of Daniel:

1. The book begins with the first Babylonian king of the exile bringing the temple vessels to Babylon (1:2) and narrates the last Babylonian king committing further sacrilege with those vessels (5:2).
2. After its introduction of Daniel and his friends to the King's court in chapter 1, the book continues with four adventure stories at the court in chapters 2–3 and in chapters 5–6, all set around a story of Nebuchadnezzar's pride in chapter 4.
3. After these four later adventure stories in chapters 2, 3, 5, and 6, the book continues with four visions related in chapters 7, 8, 9, and 10–12.
4. The stories exhibit an escalating degree of wonder and miracle, just as the visions exhibit an escalating degree of intensity and detail.

We can see than that the structure of the Hebrew and Aramaic Book of Daniel reveals a carefully planned book, one that combines structural balance with escalating poetic intensity. This structure and balance are destroyed if one assumes that the original text placed the story of Susanna at the beginning and the stories of Bel and the serpent at the end. It is clear, therefore, that these form no part of the original, even apart from the internal narrative inconsistencies involved in combining them. To say, however, that Susanna and Bel and the Serpent form no part of the original text is not to disparage them at all, for they are wonderful stories in their own right. That is why they enjoyed a literary life apart from the Book of Daniel before being appended to it.

The Story of Susanna

There was a man living in Babylon whose name was Jehoiakim. And he took a wife named Susanna, the daughter of Hilkiah, a very beautiful woman and one who feared the Lord. Her parents were righteous and had taught their daughter according to the Law of Moses. Jehoiakim was very rich and had an orchard adjoining his house, and the Jews used to come to him because he was the most honored of them all.

In that year, two elders from the people were appointed as judges. Concerning them the Lord had said, "Iniquity came forth from Babylon, from elders who were judges, who were supposed to govern the people." These men were frequently at Jehoiakim's house, and all who had cases to be tried came to them.

When the people departed at noon, Susanna would go into her husband's orchard to walk. The two elders used to watch her every day, going in and walking about, and they began to desire her. And they perverted their minds and turned away their eyes from looking to heaven or remembering righteous judgments.

Both were pierced to the heart for her, but they did not tell each other their distress, for they were ashamed to disclose their lust to possess her. And every day they watched eagerly to see her. They said to each other, "Let us go home, for it is mealtime." And when they went out, they parted from each other. But turning back, they met again; and when each pressed the other for the reason, they confessed their lust. And then together they arranged a time when they could find her alone.

Once, while they were watching for an opportune day, she went in as before with only two girls and wished to bathe in the orchard, for it was very hot. And no one was there except the two elders, hidden and watching her. She said to her girls, "Bring me oil and ointments, and shut the orchard doors so that I can bathe." They did as she said, shut the orchard doors, and went out by the side doors to bring the things they had been commanded; and they did not see the elders, because they were hidden.

When the girls had gone out, the two elders rose and ran to her, and said, "Behold, the orchard doors are shut, no one sees us, and we desire you, so give your consent and lie with us. If you refuse, we will testify against you that a young man was with you, and this was why you sent your girls away from you."

Susanna sighed deeply and said, "I am hemmed in on all sides. For if I do this thing, it is death for me; and if I do not, I will not escape your hands. I choose not to do it and to fall into your hands, rather than to sin before the Lord."

Then Susanna cried out with a loud voice, and the two elders shouted against her. And one of them ran and opened the orchard doors. When the household servants heard the shouting in the orchard, they rushed in at the side door to see what had happened to her. And when the elders spoke their words, the servants were deeply ashamed, for nothing like this had ever been said about Susanna.

The next day, when the people assembled at the house of her husband Jehoiakim, the two elders came, full of their wicked purpose to have Susanna put to death. They said before the people, "Send for Susanna, the daughter of Hilkiah, who is the wife of Jehoiakim." So they sent for her. And she came, with her parents, her children, and all her kindred.

Now Susanna was very refined and beautiful in appearance. As she was veiled, the scoundrels ordered her to be uncovered that they might feed upon her beauty. But all who were with her and all who saw her wept. Then the two elders stood up before the people and laid their hands upon her head. And she, weeping, looked up toward heaven, for her heart trusted in the Lord.

The elders said, "As we were walking in the orchard alone, this woman came in with two maids, shut the orchard doors, and dismissed the maids. Then a young man, who was hiding, came to her and lay with her. We were in a corner of the orchard, and when we saw this wickedness we ran to them. We saw them embracing, but we could not hold the man, for he was too strong for us, and he opened the doors and ran away. So we seized this woman and asked her who the young man was, but she was unwilling to tell us. These things we testify." Because they were elders of the people and judges, the assembly believed them, and they condemned her to death.

Then Susanna cried out with a loud voice and said, "O eternal God, You know what is secret and are aware of all things before they come to be. You know that these men have borne false witness against me. And now I will die, though I have done none of the things that they have wickedly invented against me!"

The Lord heard her cry. And as she was being led away to be put to death, God aroused the holy spirit of a young boy named Daniel, and he cried with a loud voice, "I am innocent of this woman's blood!"

All the people turned to him and said, "What is this thing that you said?"

Taking his stand in their midst, he said, "Are you such fools, O sons of Israel? Without examining and learning the facts, have you condemned a daughter of Israel? Return to the place of judgment. For these men have borne false witness against her."

Then all the people returned in haste. And the elders said to him, "Come, sit in our midst and inform us, for God has given you the right of an elder."

And Daniel said to them, "Separate them far from one another, and I will examine them."

When they were separated from one another, he summoned one of them and said to him, "You who have grown old in wicked days, your sins have now come, which you have committed in earlier days, pronouncing unjust judgments, condemning the innocent and setting the guilty free, though the Lord said, 'You shall not kill the innocent and righteous.' Now then, if you really saw this woman, tell me: Under what tree did you see them being intimate with each other?"

He answered, "Under a mastic tree."

And Daniel said, "Truly you have lied against your own head, for the angel of God has received the sentence from God and will immediately split you down the middle."

Then he removed him and commanded them to bring the other. And he said to him, "You seed of Canaan and not of Judah, beauty has deceived you, and lust has turned away your heart. Thus you used to treat the daughters of Israel, and they were intimate with you through fear, but a daughter of Judah would not tolerate your lawlessness. Now therefore, tell me: Under what tree did you catch them being intimate with each other?"

He answered, "Under an evergreen oak."

And Daniel said to him, "Truly you also have lied against your own head, for the angel of God is waiting with his sword to saw you down the middle, that he may destroy you both."

Then the whole assembly shouted loudly and blessed God, who saves those who hope in Him. And they rose against the two elders, for Daniel had convicted them out of their own mouth of bearing false witness, and they did to them as they had wickedly intended to do to their neighbor: acting according to the Law of Moses, they put them to death. Thus innocent blood was saved that day. And Hilkiah and his wife praised God for their daughter Susanna, and so did Jehoiakim her husband and all her kindred, because nothing shameful was found in her. And Daniel had a great reputation among the people from that day forward.

Considered on its own, *Susanna* is a wonderful tale, containing elements of sex, intrigue, danger, and mystery. It has a righteous damsel in distress, two very bad villains, a white-knight detective coming from out of nowhere to save the day at the last minute, and a satisfying ending with the villains getting what they deserved. It is, in fact, a detective story.

The story is this: In the Jewish community in exile in Babylon there lived **Susanna**, the beautiful and virtuous wife of **Jehoiakim**. The narrator skillfully prepares his ground, saying that (1) the woman was **one who feared the Lord**; (2) she lived in a house that **had an orchard adjoining** it; and (3) **the Jews used to come to** Jehoiakim there, including **two elders** of the diaspora community who were **appointed as judges**. All three elements will prove crucial to the plot. Foreshadowing of the elders' villainy comes with the Scripture citation, "**Iniquity came forth from Babylon.**"[47]

The two villainous elders of the Jewish community became infatuated with Susanna and wanted to have her. They **were frequently at Jehoiakim's house** in their capacity as judges, and the men would **watch her every day**, becoming more and more obsessed with her. They then **turned away their eyes from looking to heaven or remembering righteous judgments** (ironically, since the Law required judges to give righteous judgments). The narrator builds dramatic tension by having the judges each learn of the other's lust by accident and then throw in their lot together. This is an important plot point, for to coerce Susanna with the threat of false testimony, the witness of both of them will be required.

While they waited for their opportunity, it happened that Susanna went to her enclosure **to bathe** naked **in the orchard**. This was not her usual custom, but only because **it was very hot** that day. She had just dismissed the **girls** who waited upon her, asking them to fetch the **oil and ointments** customarily used for bathing, but they would return soon. The elders saw their chance. They ran to her and insisted that she **lie with** them. If she did not, they insisted,

---

47   No such citation can be found in the Old Testament. The narrator is probably citing the postexilic text of Zech. 5:5f, in which iniquity comes *to* Babylon.

they would both **testify against** her when the girls returned that she had just committed adultery with **a young man**, and she had **sent** the **girls away** to allow time for the forbidden tryst. At their joint testimony, she would be executed for her infidelity.

Despite this dilemma, Susanna kept her virtue, since she was indeed one who **feared the Lord**, having been **taught according to the Law of Moses**. She refused and **cried out with a loud voice** (compare Deut. 22:24). The elders **shouted** back **against her** (as if struggling with the nonexistent young lover), and **the servants rushed in at the side door** to see what all the ruckus was about. **The elders spoke their words** of accusation against Susanna, and such was their status and credibility that **the servants** believed them and were **deeply ashamed**.

The narrator skillfully shows the depths of the elders' lustful depravity by narrating a detail at the trial. When Susanna came to trial, she was of course veiled, as respectable women were in public at that time. They insisted that she **be uncovered** (a scandalous breach of decorum for one so **refined**), ostensibly to confirm that the woman was indeed Susanna, but in reality to **feed upon her beauty**. Some commentators suggest that Susanna was not merely forced to remove her veil but completely stripped. Either way, **all who saw her wept** at the depth of her humiliation. Susanna, however, **looked up toward heaven** for help—a detail the narrator deliberately mentions as a contrast to the judges, who had previously been described as having **turned away their eyes from looking to heaven**. The judges had **not remembered** the Lord's **righteous judgments**, but Susanna **trusted in the Lord** and now relied upon them.

The elders **laid their hands upon her head to accuse her** and recited their concocted story. Since they were respected judges and it was both of their words against her one, **the assembly believed** the judges and **condemned her to death**. At the verdict, Susanna **cried out** to God in prayer, and immediately **the Lord** heard her cry.

For **as she was being led away to be put to death**, at the last moment **God aroused the holy spirit of a young boy** in the crowd **named Daniel,** who had apparently been listening to the whole story. He brought the whole thing to a halt by crying out, "**I am innocent of this woman's blood!**"—that is, they were about to execute her unjustly. He insisted that all of them return to the courtroom, and he would reveal the true villain. He did this by interrogating each of the elders separately and independently, showing that their stories did not match.[48] The elders were not worried, for they were confident the stories were unshakable. They serenely invited Daniel to **come** and **sit in** their **midst**, assuming the **right** of another **elder**. Thus the narrator tells his tale like a master storyteller, building up the dramatic tension.

One gathers from Daniel's impassioned denunciation of the elders that they had been abusing the Jewish women in the community for some time, and Susanna was just the latest victim. He charges that the first elder had **grown old** throughout his many **wicked days**, **pronouncing unjust judgments, condemning the innocent and setting the guilty free**, in flagrant violation of the Law. Then comes the question (and the finally revealed importance of the alleged crime taking place in an orchard): "**Under what tree did you see them being intimate with each other?**" This was one part of their story they had not gotten straight, and he said, "**under a mastic tree**" in the garden. Daniel rejects the detail outright and convicts him as a self-confessed liar, with the curse that God's avenging **angel** would **split** him **down the middle** for his lie.

Then comes the cross-examination of the second elder. Daniel

---

48 As Proverbs declares, "He who states his case first seems right, until the other come and examines him" (Prov. 18:17).

first denounces him as a confirmed lying lecher, one who for years has abused **the daughters of Israel** like this. He is not a true seed of **Judah**, but a pagan at heart, **a seed of Canaan**! He might have coerced other **daughters of Israel** to submit to such advances, but a **daughter of Judah would not tolerate** it.[49] Daniel then asks this second elder the same question. He replies that it happened **under an evergreen oak**. An obvious lie! The same avenging **angel** was **waiting with his sword to saw** him **down the middle, that he may destroy** them **both!** It was clear to the assembly that the stories did not match and that Susanna was innocent. They **blessed God, who saves** the innocent **who hope in Him**. And they rejoiced that Daniel had saved them from shedding innocent blood. Everyone saw the two elders were lying, and they were executed in Susanna's place, according to the Law of Moses, which prescribed such retribution.

From the days of Julius Africanus (d. AD 240), many have suggested that the story was originally composed in Greek (rather than Aramaic or Hebrew) because of a pun contained in the text—a pun only apparent in Greek. Thus Daniel asks one elder under which tree the crime occurred, and he replies, "under a mastic tree" (Greek σχινον, *schinon*). Daniel retorts that God will "split" him (Greek σχισει, *schisei*) down the middle for such a lie. It is the same with the cross-examination of the other elder: when asked under which tree Susanna lay with the young man, he replies "under an evergreen oak" (Greek πρινον, *prinon*), to which Daniel responds that for such an answer God will "saw" him (Greek πρισαι, *prisai*) down the middle. It is possible (as Origen suggested to Julius in response to him pointing this out) that there could also have been a pun in the original Hebrew, but even Origen could not suggest

---

49   We detect here a postexilic polemic of the southern Judeans against their
      neighbors in the north of the land.

what such a wordplay might have been. The likelihood, therefore, is of a Greek original.

The main lesson of the story is one our culture desperately needs—the primacy of virtue. Despite Daniel's crucial role in the tale, of vindicating the accused and preventing the diaspora community from shedding innocent blood, the main hero of the story was not Daniel but Susanna. Daniel exhibited the genius of a detective, but it was Susanna who endured all the danger and had all the courage. It all came down to her simple but agonizing choice: would she choose to live by surrendering her virtue and giving in to the villains, or would she choose to maintain virtue even at the cost of her life?

We err if we too strongly equate "her virtue" with "her chastity" and read the story as solely about resisting unwanted sexual advances. The author was not solely concerned with chastity, but with virtue in general and the determination to please God by the way one lives, even if such determination comes at a great price. The life of virtue consists of more than simply chastity (though it must include it). It also includes things such as patience, kindness, self-control, truthfulness, gentleness, fairness, and modesty. It is the possession of these characteristics that should excite our admiration of people—not (as it is now) their outward beauty or their wealth or their fame.

Our culture places ultimate value not upon virtue, righteousness, and godliness, but upon the avoidance of suffering (with the experiencing of pleasure coming in at a close second place). It was otherwise in manlier and saner ages. Thoughtful people back then regarded virtue as constitutive of the good life, whether they were Christians, Jews, or pagans. For them Susanna's choice was the obvious one, even if they admitted that they might or might not have possessed the courage to make that choice. Our growth in spiritual things depends upon our recovering this ancient view on life and valuing righteousness and virtue above all other things in our culture.

Our own culture scarcely understands the true dimensions of the issues involved in the story of Susanna. It understands the value of resisting unwanted sexual advances well enough, but not because it regards sexual activity outside of marriage as immoral. Most people today would regard the advances of the men as wrong solely because they were unwanted. If Susanna had freely chosen to accept their offers of sex and decided that she wanted them, most today would conclude that no further moral dimensions were involved. If a sexual offer is welcome, it is right. It is only if it is unwelcome that it is wrong. Marital status has nothing to do with it.

For Susanna and for the people reading her story, the life of virtue included marital fidelity. Marriage in Israel involved faithfulness to one's partner, and sexual activity was sinful if engaged in outside its boundaries. Susanna had been well taught according to the Law of Moses, and she chose faithfulness to that Law even if it cost her life. Her choice challenges us today, not only to choose the virtue of chastity in an unchaste world, but also to pursue and cling to all the virtues, even if the pursuit proves to be a lonely one.

The Story of Bel and the Serpent

The stories of Bel and the Serpent (two tales in one) are also detective stories, but ones set in a pagan milieu, not within the Jewish diaspora community, and the villains are not Jews, but foolish heathen—men who insist their gods are true gods. It was a feature of exilic and postexilic Jewish polemic that the gods of the nations were dead idols, powerless to save, and that it was the height of stupidity to worship them (see the postexilic Letter of Jeremiah, sometimes found in our Bibles as chapter 6 of Baruch, with its heated denunciation of the pagan gods and its repeated refrain of "they are evidently not gods; so do not fear them").

These stories lack the narrative sensitivity and character development found in the story of Susanna and evidently come from the pen of a different author. If the Story of Susanna is a finely crafted detective story with its own dramatic tension and pathos, these tales retain a delightful element of satire and farce.

> King Astyages was gathered to his fathers, and Cyrus the Persian received his kingdom. And Daniel was a companion of the king and was honored above all of his friends.
>
> Now the Babylonians had an idol whose name was Bel, and every day they spent on it twelve bushels of fine flour and forty sheep and six vessels of wine. The king revered it and went every day to worship it. But Daniel worshiped his own God. And the king said to him, "Why do you not worship Bel?"
>
> He answered, "Because I do not revere idols made with hands but the living God, who created heaven and earth and has dominion over all flesh."
>
> The king said to him, "Do you not think that Bel is a living god? Or do you not see how much he eats and drinks every day?"
>
> Then Daniel laughed, and said, "Do not be deceived, O king; for this one is but clay inside and bronze outside, and has never eaten or drunk anything."
>
> Very angry, the king called his priests and said to them, "If you do not tell me who is eating this provision, you shall die. But if you prove that Bel eats them, Daniel shall die, because he blasphemed against Bel."
>
> And Daniel said to the king, "Let it be done as you have said."
>
> Now there were seventy priests of Bel, besides their wives and children, and the king went with Daniel into the temple of Bel. And the priests of Bel said, "Behold, we are going outside; you yourself,

O king, shall set out the food and mix and place the wine, and shut the door, and seal it with your signet. And when you return in the morning, if you do not find that Bel has eaten it all, we will die; or else Daniel will, who speaks lies about us." They were unconcerned, for under the table they had made a secret entrance, through which they used to go in regularly and consume the provisions.

When they had gone out, the king set out the food for Bel. And Daniel ordered his servants to bring ashes, and they sprinkled them throughout the whole temple in the presence of the king alone. Then they went out, shut the door, and sealed it with the king's signet, and departed. In the night the priests came with their wives and children, as they usually did, and ate and drank everything.

The king rose early the next morning and came, and Daniel with him. And the king said, "Are the seals unbroken, Daniel?"

He answered, "They are unbroken, O king." As soon as the doors were opened, the king looked at the table and shouted in a loud voice, "You are great, O Bel; and with you there is no deceit at all!"

Then Daniel laughed, and restrained the king from going in, and said, "Look at the floor, and notice whose footsteps these are."

The king said, "I see the footsteps of men, women, and children." With great anger the king seized the priests and their wives and children, and they showed him the secret doors through which they entered and consumed what was on the table. Therefore the king put them to death and gave Bel over to Daniel, who destroyed it and its temple.

The first story is set in the reign of **Cyrus the Persian**, when he had just **received his kingdom**. Daniel is described as a companion of the king, and he evidently enjoys the right of casual conversation and even rebuke. There was a great statue of the Babylonian **idol** that Cyrus revered and **went every day to worship**.[50] It is introduced to the narrative as if it were a person, for the narrator informs us that its **name was Bel**. The sacrifices offered to the idol were impressive, **for every day they spent on it twelve bushels of fine flour and forty**[51] **sheep and six vessels of wine** (this last the equivalent of about nine gallons).

Cyrus commented that Daniel should **worship Bel** too, and when Daniel declined, saying that he could only worship **the living God**, Cyrus replied that **Bel** was just as much **a living god** as Daniel's. He must be a living God, for how else, Cyrus asked, could Bel **eat and drink** so much? **Every day** an immense amount of food was put into Bel's temple for him to eat, and every morning the food was gone. Here the Jewish narrator makes no distinction between the pagan gods and their statues, and attributes to the pagans the belief that the idols actually consumed the offerings left before them. This was unhistorical, of course, but the author is penning satire and broad farce, not history.

In the narrative, Daniel was unimpressed and **laughed** at the king, declaring that the statue **had never eaten or drunk anything**. The element of Daniel's casual familiarity with the king and the freedom he feels to laugh at him, even if he was supposedly **honored above all** the king's **friends**, reveals the unhistorical nature of the tale.

Cyrus became **very angry** at the insult to his god, and eager to vindicate Bel, he called Bel's seventy priests and gave them and Daniel an ultimatum: If Bel could be shown to eat the food, Daniel would die, but if the priests could not prove that Bel ate the food, they would die. The food would be duly placed in the temple

---

50 It is more likely that Cyrus's main devotion was to the Zoroastrian Ahura Mazda, not the Babylonian Marduk/Bel.

51 Thus the later Theodotian reading; the Old Greek text reads "four sheep."

and the doors to the temple locked and **sealed with** the king's **signet** so no one could sneak in to eat the food. When they unlocked the temple and looked in the next morning, either Bel would have eaten the food or it would be left uneaten, and that way everyone would know whether or not Bel actually ate all that food. Daniel was serene, trusting that all would be well.

The priests also **were unconcerned**, for **under the table they had made a secret entrance** into the temple, and every night they and their families would sneak into the temple when no one was there, eat the food, and leave. This they planned to do again that night. What they did not know was that before the temple doors were locked for the night, after they had left, **Daniel** had **ordered his servants to bring ashes,** which they secretly **sprinkled** all over the floor **throughout the whole temple in the presence of the king alone**.

When morning came, Cyrus asked Daniel if **the seals** to the temple were **unbroken**. When Daniel affirmed that they were, Cyrus looked into the temple, saw that the food had been eaten (obviously by Bel), and triumphantly called out to his god, "**You are great, O Bel, and with you is no deceit!**" The narrator deliberately puts these words on the king's lips, knowing that the worship of Bel and the idols was nothing but deceit—as Daniel was about to reveal.

At the king's elated cry, **Daniel laughed** once again at his king's credulity, **restrained** him **from going in** and disturbing the evidence, and pointed out the footprints left by the priests and their families in the ashes, which they had not seen on the floor because it was dark. The king knew then that his priests had lied, and once they revealed how the ruse with **the secret doors** had worked, the king therefore **put them to death** and **gave** the idol **Bel over to Daniel, who destroyed** both **it and its temple**. The implausibility of Cyrus killing his own priests and allowing Daniel to destroy both the image of Bel and its temple once again reveals the unhistorical nature of the world in which the tale is set.

> There was also a great serpent, which the Babylonians revered. And the king said to Daniel, "You cannot say that this is not a living god; so worship it!"
>
> Daniel said, "I will worship the Lord my God, for he is the living God. But, O king, give me permission, and I will slay the serpent without sword or club."
>
> The king said, "I give you permission."
>
> Then Daniel took pitch, fat, and hair, and boiled them and made cakes, which he fed to the serpent. The serpent ate them and burst open. And Daniel said, "Behold what you have been worshiping!"
>
> When the Babylonians heard it, they were indignant and conspired against the king, saying, "The king has become a Jew! He has destroyed Bel, and slain the serpent, and slaughtered the priests!"
>
> Going to the king, they said, "Deliver Daniel to us, or we will kill you and your household!" The king saw that they were pressing him hard, and under compulsion he delivered Daniel to them.
>
> They threw Daniel into the lions' den, and he was there for six days. There were seven lions in the den, and every day they had been given two bodies and two sheep, but these things were not given to them now, that they might devour Daniel.
>
> Now the prophet Habakkuk was in Judea. He had made a stew and had broken bread into a bowl, and was going into the field to take it to the reapers. But the angel of the Lord said to Habakkuk, "Take the dinner you have into Babylon to Daniel, who is in the lions' den."
>
> Habakkuk said, "Lord, I have never seen Babylon, nor do I know the den."
>
> Then the angel of the Lord took him by the crown of his head,

and carried him by his hair and set him down in Babylon, right
over the den, with the speed of the wind. Then Habakkuk cried out,
"Daniel, Daniel! Take the meal which God has sent you."

And Daniel said, "You have remembered me, O God, and have
not forsaken those who love You." So Daniel arose and ate. And
the angel of God immediately returned Habakkuk to his place.

On the seventh day, the king came to mourn Daniel. When he
came to the den, he looked in, and there sat Daniel. And the king
cried out with a loud voice, "Great are You, O Lord God of Daniel,
and there is no other besides You!" And he pulled Daniel out, and
threw into the den the men who had plotted his destruction, and
they were devoured immediately before his face.

In the second story of the two-act drama, we meet **a great serpent**,
kept in a zoo of sorts and worshipped as a god. The element of
broad comedy continues. Here, said Cyrus again to Daniel (smarting as he was after suffering humiliation in the matter of Bel), **"You
cannot say that this is not a living god; so worship it!"** Daniel
was not impressed by this claim either and offered to demonstrate
that the snake was not a living and immortal god by killing it **without sword or club**. The king said he could try, wondering how one
might kill a snake without such weapons.

The battle of wits had begun again, but it was no problem for
Daniel: he **took pitch, fat, and hair, boiled them and made** them
into **cakes**. The snake ate the cakes, not knowing what they contained, after which he naturally burst open and died, thereby proving he was not a god after all. The challenge ended with the trium-
phant polemic of Daniel to the hapless king: **"Behold what you
have been worshiping!"** The narrator here addresses all the pagans
of the world, rebuking them for their naïve stupidity.

This story, however, has a second act: After Daniel killed their
snake, the Babylonians heard it and were indignant, saying, **"The**

king has become a Jew! He has destroyed Bel, and slain the serpent, and slaughtered the priests!"[52] They then mobbed the king,
demanding that he deliver Daniel to them or they would kill him
and his household. Scared for his life, the king did so, and they
threw Daniel into the lions' den for six days.[53] The lions had been
accustomed to a grisly daily meal of two dead bodies and two sheep,
but they had been deprived of this and starved so that they might
more surely devour Daniel.

Meanwhile, an **angel of the Lord** appeared to the prophet
Habakkuk, who was back in Judea, where he had just **broken
bread** into a **bowl** of **stew**, preparing to take it to the men reaping
his fields. The angel told him instead to take the supper to Daniel in the lions' den in Babylon.[54] Habakkuk replied that he had
never seen Babylon and couldn't find his way to **the den** mentioned, whereupon an angel **carried him by his hair** to Babylon[55]
and hovered **over the den**. Daniel thanked God for the food, and
the angel, having delivered the supper, **returned Habakkuk** to his
home. Daniel **arose and ate** the supper, so that his week in the den
was not a hungry time at all.

When the king came and found that the lions had not touched
Daniel all week, he cried out, **"Great are You, O Lord God of
Daniel, and there is no other besides You!"** The Babylonians
were right: the king had become a Jew after all (compare Is. 45:18;
46:9). Moreover, he then threw into the den those who tried to
destroy Daniel, and the lions **devoured** them **before his face**. It is

---

52 We see in this language the anti-Semitic confrontations of a time later than
    the exile.
53 We note in passing the historical implausibility of the entire scenario.
54 The narrator does not need to inform us that the lions did not in fact devour
    Daniel; he expects his listeners to know this already, being familiar with
    chapter six of the canonical Book of Daniel.
55 A detail modeled on Ezek. 8:3, though there Ezekiel is carried in a vision, not
    physically (as here).

essential in these tales that the villains are suitably punished: the wicked elders in the story of Susanna are executed in her place, the priests of Bel are put to death, and those throwing Daniel to the lions are themselves eaten by the lions in his place. The Jewish *lex talionis*, or law of just retribution, can be observed in all these punishments.

Even apart from the problems with the dates (Habakkuk prophesied while the temple was still standing, prior to 587 BC, probably about 600 BC, not during the exile[56]), the lack of historicity is apparent. The author of the tales evidently was familiar with the original Book of Daniel and adapted the story of Nebuchadnezzar's image and of Darius (not Cyrus!) at the lions' den for his own use, increasing Daniel's stay in the den from overnight to one week.

One also notices a lack of sophistication in the polemic. Pagans of that day did not imagine that the statues of their gods actually ate the offerings made to them, nor that animals sacred to their gods (such as serpents or crocodiles) were actually divine and immortal themselves. One should not read these stories for information about the pagan beliefs of the ancient world, nor even to learn about how Israel thought the pagans believed. Rather, the value of the tales lies in their satire.

Israel felt itself surrounded by pagan neighbors, nations that were bigger, richer, more powerful, and better armed than themselves. Their temples were big and impressive, well funded and secure, and the worship of pagan deities was spread throughout the world. Wherever in the world one went, one found a multiplicity of pagan gods and their statues, grand temples and busy altars, and a

---

56 It appears that the author chose Habakkuk as his exilic prophet because of the prophet's reference to "the Chaldeans" in Hab. 1:6. Like many in his day, the author had but a minimal understanding of history and chronology for events long past.

well-funded priesthood offering sacrifices. What was little Jerusalem and her shrine in comparison?

A Jew from the time of the exile and afterward, when they had regained the land and rebuilt their temple, might be tempted to view his own temple and religion as paltry in comparison, or at least as second rate. Especially with the rise of Hellenism as a force across the Middle East, Jews knew their ancestral faith was only one of many options in the marketplace of the world. The pagans derided them for their religion. Might the pagans be right after all?

Wherever Jews looked in the world, they beheld huge crowds thronging about the pagan temples and placing offerings before beautifully adorned statues of gold and silver. The images of the gods shone under the sun and enticed the heart. It was urgently necessary to remove the sheen from the religion of the pagans and to remove the numinous quality from the whole spectacle.

We see one such attempt in the words of Isaiah 44. Here the prophet takes the listener step-by-step through the whole process of creating a pagan statue, from the hewing down of the tree to the carving of the image. Isaiah also portrays the process of making the statue in 40:18–20 and 41:7, describing the labor of the goldsmith soldering on the plates of gold and fastening it with nails. By detailing this behind-the-scenes look at the creation of the image, the prophet allows the listener to reflect that after all is said and done, the impressive shining image is just an artifact, like anything else that can be made and sold. The prophet's intention is not to offer a thoughtful critique of pagan theology, much less a reasoned defense of Jewish monotheism, but simply to debunk pagan mysticism.

The stories of Bel and the Serpent were written within the same tradition, though here the author writes not to debunk but to deride. He writes farce, comedy, satire. In the ideological war of Israel's ancestral faith and the pagan alternatives, the author encourages his countrymen by allowing them to laugh at the insanity which is idolatry.

The project resembles that of America's wartime propaganda assault on Nazi Germany by Charlie Chaplin in his 1940 movie *The Great Dictator*. This film was not intended as a thoughtful response to the principles of National Socialism, but as an attempt to mock Hitler and thereby neutralize the spectacle of Nazi pomp. The Nuremburg rallies and the Riefenstahl film *Triumph of the Will* were intended to show Hitler's invincibility and make his enemies quake. Chaplin answered with the film *The Great Dictator* to prove that no one there was quaking. In the same spirit, Bel and the Serpent provided faithful Jews with the opportunity to mock and laugh at pagan pomp and show that they refused to quake. They could turn from the complex colors of the heathen world back to the sanity that was Israel's ancestral faith in the living God.

CONCLUSION

Final Reflections

In this final section we offer a number of reflections, as well as conclusions drawn from preceding commentary. We have attempted to listen to the Book of Daniel with the heart of a child, hearing the stories as they were intended to be heard, without the filters provided by polemicists, either liberal or conservative. We now will attempt a more detailed synthesis of the material and its conclusions.

The Four Empires and the Culmination of the Kingdoms

The four empires examined throughout the Book of Daniel may be listed as the Assyrian/Babylonian, the Median, the Persian, and the Macedonian/Greek. This last developed into the four power centers that arose from Alexander's empire, of which the Seleucid and the Egyptian had the greatest direct impact on the Jews of Palestine. For the Jews of the second century B.C., this succession of empires culminated in the Seleucid kingdom and its king, Antiochus IV Epiphanes.

We identify these four empires by examining the visions found in chapters two, seven, eight, nine, and ten to twelve. In those chapters we first identify the *Assyrian/Babylonian kingdom*. It is symbolized in chapter two by the head of gold, identified with King Nebuchadnezzar (vv. 32, 38), who ruled Babylon. (It was the Babylonians, together with the Medes, who conquered the Assyrian capital of Nineveh in 612 BC and soon after inherited its empire and power.)

In chapter seven, the Assyrian/Babylonian kingdom is symbolized by the beast that was like a lion with eagles' wings (vv. 4f). There is little scholarly debate over this identification.

We next identity the *Median kingdom*, symbolized in chapter two by the breast and arms of silver (vv. 32, 39), and in chapter seven by the beast like a bear (v. 5). This identification does not necessarily involve asserting that the Medes had an independent existence between the Babylonian empire and the Persian one; only that there was a distinct kingdom of the Medes, and that it was inferior in power to the Babylonians (2:39). The Medes' connection with the next empire, the Persian one, is expressed by the ram of chapter eight representing both the Medes and the Persians (v. 20).

The third empire was the *Persian kingdom*, symbolized in chapter two by the image's bronze belly and thighs (vv. 32, 39), in chapter seven by the winged leopard (v. 6), and in chapter eight by the ram with the two horns (v. 3).

The fourth empire was the *Macedonian or Greek kingdom* established by the whirlwind conquests of Alexander the Great, symbolized in chapter two by the legs of iron on Nebuchadnezzar's image (vv. 33, 40), in chapter seven by the nameless fourth beast (v. 7), and in chapter eight by the he-goat (v. 5). With this fourth kingdom, the narrator closes in on concerns more central to his own time, the kingdom of the Seleucids, symbolized in Nebuchadnezzar's image by feet of iron and clay (2:33, 41), and by the ten horns on the fourth beast (7:7f).

That is why the narration in chapter eight skips over the Babylonian kingdom and begins with the combined Medo-Persian one, for the Persians were the reigning world power when Alexander took aim at them and invaded Asia Minor in 334 BC, overthrowing the main Persian army of Darius III the next year. It is also why the detailed vision of the end in chapters eleven to twelve omits any

Babylonian events and begins with Persian events (summed up in a single verse), and also why it summarizes the career of Alexander in a single verse—the narrator hurries along to his central concern, which is the powers that grew out of the shattered Greek empire and gave birth to the Seleucid power of Antiochus Epiphanes.

We also see how all the visions culminate in the coming and challenge of Antiochus the persecutor. The vision of Nebuchadnezzar's image traces all four empires down to the iron kingdom of the Greeks and its ten Seleucid toes, culminating when the supernatural stone of God hits the ten toes and shatters the image to bits (2:34f). The vision of the four beasts traces all four empires down to the fourth Greek beast with its ten horns. It culminates in the rise of a little horn speaking words against the Most High, warring against the saints, and changing times and law until he is finally destroyed by the supernatural power of God (7:25f).

The vision of the ram and the he-goat narrows its focus and traces the fall of the Medo-Persian empire to the Greek one, again culminating with the rise of a little horn speaking words against the Most High, warring against the saints, and removing the daily sacrifice (tamid) until he is destroyed by the supernatural power of God (8:9f).

The vision of the seventy weeks takes the listener from the time of Jeremiah's initial prophecy down to the time of its absolutely final fulfillment, culminating in the assassination of a high priest, the removal of the sacrifice, and the setting up of the abomination of desolation until the desolator is destroyed (9:26–27). The final vision of the end traces the history of Israel from the Persian empire down to Antiochus Epiphanes, who speaks words against the Most High, wars against the saints, removes the daily sacrifice, and sets up the abomination of desolation until he is finally destroyed (11:31f). This culmination is mentioned again in the final epilogue in 12:11f, when Antiochus's removal of the daily sacrifice and setting up the abomination of desolation marks the end of Israel's suffering. In all these visions, we see the identical pattern and the same culmination—that of Antiochus Epiphanes and his blasphemous substitution of the abomination of desolation for the daily sacrifice.

We also see a pattern of increasing detail as the visions follow in sequence. In chapter two, we find only four empires, the only detail being one relating to the fourth empire, where it is said that the iron and clay attempting to mix together is an image for dynasties attempting to combine through marriage (such as occurred between the Egyptian and Seleucid kingdoms arising from the Greek kingdom). In chapter seven we see more detail about the first three kingdoms, and even more detail about the fourth, where it is said that the little horn speaks words against God, wears out the saints of the Most High, and changes the times and law.

More detail comes in chapter eight, where we learn that the little horn changes the times and law by removing the daily sacrifice. Yet more detail comes with chapter nine, where we learn that the desolator causes the sacrifice to cease for three and a half years. Then in the final vision, the narrator dispenses with symbols altogether and speaks of the king of the North's career (including his removal of the daily sacrifice and setting up of the abomination of desolation) in such detail as to enable his positive identification as Antiochus IV Epiphanes. Given the pattern of parallelism in the visions, no other identifications are possible.

Not that other identifications haven't been tried. We mention but a few.

One school of interpretation identifies the fourth empire not as Greek, but as the Roman Empire. This view is as old as 2 Esdras, as we have seen. But there are problems with this identification. Those objecting to identifying the fourth kingdom with the Greek kingdom point out that the Greek kingdom has passed away, and yet the end has not come. But that can be said also about the Roman Empire, which has also passed away, and yet the eternal Kingdom has not come. This interpretation also has to assert that the little horn of chapter seven is completely different from the little horn of chapter eight, despite the fact that they both act in the same way—changing the law, speaking against God, and persecuting His people.

This school of interpretation often interprets the vision of the seventy weeks as culminating not with Antiochus Epiphanes as the one who causes offering to cease, but with Jesus Christ. There are several problems with this, one of which is that with the death of Jesus, offering in the temple did not in fact cease. It continued for another forty years until the Romans destroyed the temple in AD 70. Until that time the sacrifices continued to be offered, and even the apostles offered sacrifice there (Acts 21:23f). Saying the sacrifices had been made superfluous by the death of Christ (see Heb. 8:13) is not the same thing as saying they had actually ceased. More importantly, throughout the rest of the Book of Daniel (in chapters eight, eleven, and twelve), the cessation of the sacrifices is regarded as the supreme calamity, so it is impossible to regard the predicted cessation in chapter nine as something to be celebrated. This alone disqualifies the Lord Jesus as the referent in chapter nine.

The main difficulty with all these interpretations is the violence they do to the parallel patterns and structure of the Book of Daniel. If these rival interpretations are correct, chapter two culminates in the end of the age (somehow identified with the end of the Roman Empire, despite its long disappearance from history). Chapter seven does likewise; chapter eight culminates with Antiochus Epiphanes in the second century BC; chapter nine culminates with Jesus Christ in the middle of the first century AD; chapter ten refers to Antiochus Epiphanes in the middle of the chapter and then jumps to the end of the world in chapter twelve, before ending with Antiochus Epiphanes again at the book's conclusion—this despite the fact that each chapter culminates with a little horn who speaks words against God, persecutes God's people, and removes the daily sacrifice. Surely any sensible interpretation will regard all these chapters as culminating with the same man and the same events.

All the adventure stories in the Book of Daniel offer the lesson that a Jew must remain faithful to his ancestral traditions and disregard the pompous pride of pagan kings. All the visions culminate with the persecution of Antiochus Epiphanes, when these lessons were urgently needed. It is difficult to deny the conclusion that this was all because the book was written during and for this time.

The Date of the Book of Daniel

We have suggested throughout this commentary that the Book of Daniel is not an historical record and a collection of predictions dating from the sixth century BC, but rather a pseudepigraphal apocalypse dating from the second century, possibly incorporating material from an earlier time. A number of factors push one to this conclusion.

First of all, we find the historical material contained in the stories set in Babylon does not match history, as we mentioned in the footnotes. Such a view of history as we find there makes no sense if written by a contemporary eyewitness of the events in the sixth century BC, but might be expected of someone writing in the second century, for to that person the events would be long past, and many of the common people in Palestine would have only a vague historical grasp of those ancient events. The common man did not have such access to historical records as we do today, and such confusions would not be unusual.

Attempts to salvage the historicity of the adventure stories have not been successful, though its defenders have valiantly offered a variety of (mutually incompatible) solutions. Darius the Mede, for example, has been identified by the defenders of historicity with people as various as Cambyses, Ugbaru (Cyrus's governor), Astyges, Cyaxares, and even Cyrus the Persian himself. Such variety witnesses to an element of desperation on the part of the defenders and to the impossibility of the attempt.

Added to the seemingly cloudy view and uncertain grip on sixth-century history is a completely accurate and finely detailed view of second-century history. It is the *combination* of an unclear view of the Babylonian times with an apparent intimate acquaintance with Hellenistic times that leads one to conclude that the writer was in fact living in those Hellenistic times. Otherwise, how would one explain a sixth-century writer's uncertain grip on his own times and his apparent obsession with the Hellenistic period? It is of course possible that a prescient sixth-century prophet would focus with such detail on Antiochus Epiphanes to the exclusion of everything else (including the destruction of the temple by Rome in AD 70), but such a narrow concern needs explaining.

We also note the vocabulary of the book. It may (or may not) be true that the Aramaic used is compatible with that used in the sixth century. But it appears that the Hebrew used has more in common with the postexilic Hebrew of Ezra and afterward than it does with Late Biblical Hebrew, such as was used in the exile. Add to this the presence of Greek words (such as those describing the musical instruments in chapter two) which date from Hellenistic times, and the impression of a Hellenistic date for the book is strengthened.

Additionally, in the Hebrew canon the Book of Daniel is listed not among the Prophets but among the Writings. This may indicate a late date, since it was considered by the Jews that the period of prophecy ceased with the prophet Malachi, in about 400 BC.

Also, we cannot find Daniel listed among the prophets in the long description in praise of famous biblical men in Sirach 44—50. The roll of Hebrew heroes follows a roughly chronological path, so that if Daniel were known to be the great prophet and seer of the exile, one would expect to find him described after Ezekiel and before Zerubbabel in Sirach 49, but in fact Daniel never shows up anywhere at all. This may indicate a date for the Book of Daniel after the Book of Sirach was written. At the very least, the omission needs some explanation if the Book of Daniel was written in the sixth century and known in Israel afterward.

None of the many and varied arguments for a late date for Daniel is conclusive in itself. But when they are taken together, the cumulative effect is overwhelming. The defenders of an early date are driven to their positions not so much by the objective evidence, but by their prior ideological commitment to the historicity of the Book of Daniel. For them, Daniel claims to be historically accurate and claims to be predictive prophecy. And since it is part of the canonical Word of God, it must be historically accurate and genuine prophecy, all evidence to the contrary notwithstanding.

We therefore turn next to examine the issue of literary genre.

Literary Genre and History in the Book of Daniel

In discussing the literary genre of the Book of Daniel and the question of whether or not it claims to be writing history, we must first examine what we mean by "history," for the ancients did not write history as we do today. Today we rigorously distinguish in our reporting between "the facts" (presented objectively on the front page of the newspaper) and the editorial/opinion piece (presented as such inside the newspaper on page eleven). In presenting "the facts," no editorial liberty is allowed: if one hundred people showed up at an event, we cannot stretch the number to two hundred or one thousand. If we report what a person said, we must quote him accurately and verbatim, with no paraphrasing or invention of words ascribed to him, even though it's the sort of thing the speaker always says at such gatherings. If we diverge from these norms, the paper must either print a retraction or risk being sued. That is history as understood by us moderns.

It was otherwise with the ancients in their reportage. For them the aim was not to report speeches verbatim or to use numbers with mathematical accuracy. For them it was mostly about *truth*—not simply giving the facts, but giving the person listening to the report an understanding of the significance of what had happened. What we have separated into the two categories of "history" and "interpretation" was for them the same activity. That is why their use of numbers, for example, was sometimes more poetic and symbolical than is our use today. To *us* it seems they were using numbers too loosely and being bad historians. As far as they were concerned, they were just letting people know the whole truth, what truth felt like to those involved, and what it all meant. *We* think they were too lax in their historical reporting; *they* would have said we are too pedantic and constricted in ours. There is nothing wrong with either approach, of course; one just needs to know what one is actually doing and not foist standards onto the other approach that do not really apply.

Historical reporting therefore was primarily *storytelling*, containing both objective facts and historical imagination, often on a sliding scale of proportions. Sometimes (such as in 1–2 Samuel and 1–2 Kings) the amount of imagination is very low; sometimes (such as in 1–2 Chronicles) it is rather higher. That accounts for the differences between the two accounts when they report the same events. We err when we apply our own standards of accuracy to these histories and try to make them both conform to our modern norms, sandpapering away the differences and trying to cram the bigger material of 1–2 Chronicles into the smaller suitcase of 1–2 Kings.

So then: Does the Book of Daniel claim to be writing history? Or is it another genre, such as an historical romance? We moderns talk about different historical genres and differentiate between history on the one hand and historical romance/historical fiction on the other. That is helpful to us, but in discussing this we must recognize that it is doubtful the ancients would recognize our distinction as meaningful. For them, what we call an historical romance was simply a story with a high degree of imagination and a low degree of actual occurrence. Take such historical romances as the Book of Tobit or (better yet) the Book of Judith.

In the story of Judith, we find that Nebuchadnezzar (called the king of the Assyrians, not the Babylonians) was in a furious rage, and through his general Holofernes he had plundered the nations and destroyed their temples. Holofernes had now invaded Judea, where the people lived in peace, having "only recently returned from the captivity" along with "the sacred vessels and the altar and the temple [which had] been consecrated after their profanation" (Jud. 4:3). To us moderns, this is proof that we are not reading history, but historical romance, for after the return from captivity and the reconsecration of the temple, Nebuchadnezzar was long gone.

Yet the Book of Judith opens and is replete with historical details (often incorrect ones), such as, "In the twelfth year of the reign of Nebuchadnezzar who ruled over the Assyrians in the great city of Nineveh, in the days of Arphaxad who ruled over the Medes in Ecbatana . . ." (Jud. 1:1). It feels like history—and that is the point. Such historical verisimilitude was essential to the telling of a good story. But was it fiction? The ancients, I think, would have answered that the story was true—for the story was not about Nebuchadnezzar or even about Holofernes, but about courage, heroism, patriotism, and faithfulness to the Law. Judith's qualities and her actions made the story a true one. We listen to the tale and are meant to conclude, "that is how I should live," not "this is not a true story, because Holofernes and Judith never really existed." To truly appreciate these ancient writings, we must learn to read them as the ancients did and to speak two languages—both our modern critical one and the ancient devotional one.

The Book of Daniel is more like the Book of Judith than it is like 1–2 Kings. It tells stories about adventures and visions in Babylon. Like the Book of Judith, its aim is to tell its listeners how to live, not simply to present them with factoids about ancient occurrences.

It seems clear, given its literary characteristics and its use of history, that the Book of Daniel should not be read like a history (especially as we define it today), but as historical romance or fiction. Realizing this means there are no "mistakes" or historical errors in the Book of Daniel. Talking about mistakes in Daniel would be like talking about mistakes in our Lord's parable of the Prodigal Son, because the prodigal son "never really existed." The point of the parable is not its historicity but its lesson of truth.

In the Book of Daniel, the author takes history as understood by the common man of his day (containing what to us moderns are "historical errors") and uses it as the framework for the lessons he wants to convey. The common man then doubtless had an imperfect grasp of ancient history, and it was not the author's concern to correct it even if he could. His aim was to correct not a view of ancient history, but the trajectory of the heart—to inflame his listener with the love of God and steel him to resist infidelity and endure persecution for the sake of his faith.[57]

---

57 We note the same thing in our Lord's teaching: the common man in His time thought that the one who was slain between the sanctuary and the altar in ancient times was "Zechariah the son of Barachiah" (Matt. 23:35), when in

Ardent and well-intentioned defenders of Daniel's historicity often assert that Daniel "purports to be serious history."[58] Reading the book as we have suggested, with the wide eyes of a child, tells a different story: Daniel in fact purports to contain larger-than-life adventures, with an earth-shattering, life-changing message that cannot wait. Historical details such as, "In the third year of the reign of Jehoiakim the king of Judah, Nebuchadnezzar king of Babylon came to Jerusalem and besieged it" (Dan. 1:1) do not prove that it "purports to be serious history" any more than a similar opening for the Book of Judith proves that *it* purports to be serious history. Historical verisimilitude always feels like history by definition; that is its function.

It is sometimes difficult for conservative-minded Christians today to accept such an approach. Our culture trains us to equate "true" with "historically accurate according to modern standards of accuracy," and since the Church teaches that the Bible narratives are "true," we conclude they must somehow conform to our modern standards of historical accuracy and reporting. When they do not, we are upset and strive mightily to make them conform to those standards, even sometimes at the cost of making the text say what it in fact does not say (such as, for example, regarding the height of Nebuchadnezzar's image in chapter three). But the truth of the Scriptures does not consist of their conformity to modern norms of accuracy, but in the eternal reliability of their message, which is in turn rooted in their divine origin. Thus the Bible's narratives are true even when they conform to ancient standards of historical

---

fact it was Zechariah the son of Jehoidah (2 Chron. 24:20f). Our Lord did not "make a mistake"; He was simply assuming the historicity of what His hearers thought and using their terms of reference. He was not concerned to fine-tune their history, but to warn them of the wrath to come.

58   E.g., E. J. Young, in his *The Prophecy of Daniel* (Grand Rapids: Eerdmans, 1949), p. 25.

reporting rather than ours (which, after all, is only to be expected in ancient writings).

The difficulty for some in accepting this approach to the Book of Daniel is compounded because we sometimes find it difficult to accept that the Scriptures use a variety of literary genres, some of which have higher degrees of historical accuracy (as defined by us moderns) than others. We tend to think of the Scriptural collection as a single volume, since "the Bible" is a singular noun, not a plural one (despite the fact that the term is derived from the Greek *ta biblia*, "the books"). But even though the Bible is bound within a single set of covers with its texts arranged in an identical way (possibly with two columns per page), the Bible is in fact not a single book, but a library, consisting of many books written by many authors over centuries. It is hardly surprising that the books are of differing literary genres. Some of the books represent a more historical genre (such as 1–2 Kings), while others are historical romance (such as the Book of Judith). And all of them are true.

We need to open our heart when we read the Book of Daniel (and the rest of the Scriptures) and let it work in us with its own power. As with the rest of the Bible, we come to the Book of Daniel on our knees and listen to the Word of God with trembling. It has a life-changing message for us no less than for its original hearers, and we must do our best to take it in—not nitpick over details like the historicity of Darius the Mede. The Book of Daniel is God's Word, and God's Word is so big and rich that it uses many historical genres—including historical romance.

But Wasn't Its Apocalyptic Timetable Wrong?

Throughout our study in the Book of Daniel, we have noted that the sweep of history in all the visions culminated with the final conflict with Antiochus Epiphanes, and that the Kingdom of God and a resurrection from the dust of death to eternal life could be expected then (12:2). But, one might ask, hasn't history proven such a timetable wrong and its hope misplaced? It is one thing to recognize that one should not apply modern historical standards of accuracy to the adventure stories of the Book of Daniel; it is something else again to accept an apocalyptic timetable that has been proven to be wrong. In examining this question, we must look more closely at the apocalyptic genre itself and attempt to read it as the ancients did and not as we moderns might. The apocalyptic genre was not an ancient example of Hal Lindsey's *The Late, Great Planet Earth*.[59]

The Book of Daniel was an early example of the apocalyptic, but there were many others written around that time. The *Book of Enoch*, for example, purported to represent the revelations made to Enoch (who lived seven generations from Adam; Gen. 5:24) regarding those "who will be living in the day of tribulation, when all the wicked and godless are to be removed" (Enoch 1:1). The Book of 2 Esdras (sometimes called "4 Ezra") is another example. It purports to be the work of Ezra, whom it identifies with the postexilic Shealtiel (2 Esdras 3:1). In it Ezra is given dreams and visions by angels, including one of an eagle with twelve wings and three heads (2 Esdras 11:1). Towards end of the book, Ezra is told to present the canonical Scriptures to all the people, but to seal up and keep these revelations hidden, and to give them only to the wise at the end time (2 Esdras 12:36–38; 14:44–48). The genre flourished during the centuries immediately before Christ. The New Testament Epistle of Jude quotes from one of them.[60]

Obviously these apocalyptic books were not written by their

---

59   Published in 1970, the bestseller was one of many such books purporting to predict the final end-time events in detail leading up to "the Rapture" and the Second Coming of Christ.

60   Jude 14 quotes from Enoch 1:9.

purported authors. Having an ancient worthy or sage as the sup-posed author was a literary convention of the genre, one which added to the authority of the visions and the message generally. It was not so much an attempt to deceive the readership as an identi-fication with an ancient tradition of wisdom (in the same way that *The Wisdom of Solomon* was ascribed to Solomon; he didn't actually write it, but the book contained things so wise that Solomon him-self might have said them).

One characteristic common to these apocalypses is a call to action for the people of God, preparing them for the imminent end. All of these works present the end as if it were at hand, so that the immi-nence of the end of the age is an invariable part of the genre. If one regards the genre as primarily concerned with timetables and calen-dars, then the apocalyptic authors were indeed mistaken and their timetables wrong. But that is not how the genre works, nor how we should read it. Their main message was not "in a year or two the end of the world will come," but "be wise enough to resist secular-ism and prepare yourselves for the final judgment." They conveyed this message by presenting their audience with a supposedly ancient tradition of visions and a timetable warning of the imminent end. But the timetable was never the point; the preparation of the heart and the wisdom was. It is true that the timetable was incorrect, but the timetable was only ever a way of presenting the message; it was never the message itself.

In reading apocalyptic literature, one needs to step back to take in the whole panoramic sweep of the message, not put one's nose so close to the fine details that one misses the message, unable to see the forest for the trees. Once again we may be tempted to make historical accuracy into an idol and miss the real point. The literary convention of ancient authorship and the timetable culminating in the end of the world were simply the author's way of getting across his message, like the details of a parable. The parable never was about such details, but about how the people of God should prepare their hearts.

In this the authors of apocalypses were not so different from the authors of our New Testament. The apostles also spoke of the imminent end of the world: "The Lord is at hand!" (Phil. 4:5). "The Judge is standing at the door!" (James 5:9). "The end of all things is at hand" (1 Peter 4:7). "Children, it is the last hour" (1 John 2:18). "Surely, I am coming soon!" (Rev. 22:20). The apostles were not wrong in writing these things, for they were not predicting the future any more than were the writers of the apocalyptic books in the centuries before them. Both the apostles and the apocalypticists were proclaiming the eschatological nature of the times in which they lived—and in which we continue to live today. The apostles were telling us that the Kingdom of Christ is ready to break in, and we must be ready for it. In the centuries immediately before Christ, the writers of apocalyptic literature were doing the same. We misread their work if we focus all our attention on the accuracy or otherwise of their timetables. The timetable was just the envelope containing their real message. That message was "The Lord is at hand," and they were not wrong.

What About Daniel?

Given that the Book of Daniel was a pseudepigraphal and early apocalyptic work, must we conclude there was no such person as Daniel? This seems unlikely, given that the apocalyptic writers' habit was to ascribe their works to ancient worthies, not to make up mythological characters out of whole cloth. In fact, we hear of a Daniel in the prophecies of Ezekiel, in a passage where he is grouped with Noah and Job as the most righteous men on earth: "Even if these three men, Noah, Daniel, and Job, were in [the sinful land of Israel] they would deliver but their own lives by their righteousness, says the Lord Yahweh" (Ezek. 14:14). Also in Ezekiel 28:3–4, denouncing the prince of Tyre for his pride: "You are indeed wiser than Daniel; no secret is hidden from you; by your wisdom and your understanding you have gotten wealth for yourself."

Whoever this Daniel is, Ezekiel at the time of the exile considered him as a man of righteousness and wisdom. There are, however, problems with connecting this Daniel with the man portrayed in the Book of Daniel. Firstly, the name is spelled not like the Daniel in our book, but "Danel" (lacking the Hebrew letter *yod*, or "i"). Some have connected the name to King Danel in the Ugaritic literature, a non-Israelite king of antiquity famous for judging the widow and saving the orphan. Another problem is that the "Danel" of Ezekiel 14 is placed in the middle of other ancient non-Israelites such as Noah and Job. Some have pointed out the oddness of Ezekiel putting a contemporary exilic figure into the midst of such ancient figures. They have also wondered how a young exile like Daniel came to be so quickly regarded as a venerable sage that he could be numbered with Noah and Job in the mind of his contemporary Ezekiel. It is possible, therefore, that the Danel of Ezekiel had no connection with anyone in the exile, however the name was spelled.

But all of this still leaves unexplained how someone in later, possibly Hellenistic, times would choose the name Daniel for the person living in the exile to whom the work could be ascribed. An ancient pagan king mentioned in Ugaritic literature with no connection to the exile seems an unlikely candidate. If our book follows the later classic apocalyptic pattern of pseudepigraphy, then it seems as if some Jewish exile named Daniel reached a position of prominence in Babylon and had enough of a reputation for wisdom to provide the appropriate name to which to ascribe such a work.[61]

---

61 Alternatively, one could say that the Book of Daniel, as an early example of

The fact that no genealogy is given for Daniel (unlike Ezra; compare Ezra 7:1f) suggests that not much else was known about him apart from this reputation.[62]

The Book of Daniel and Christology

What then does the Book of Daniel tell us about the Lord Jesus Christ? If it was not intended as a direct prophecy and prediction of His coming, has it no Christological significance at all? The Book of Daniel, like all the rest of the Old Testament, speaks about Jesus Christ, and does so in the same way as the rest of the Old Testament.[63] The Old Testament speaks about Christ not through direct prediction, but through poetry—a poetry inspired by the Spirit of God and so imbued with special hidden meanings that could only be understood in light of their fulfillment. The poetry is thus also prophecy. We take two examples to illustrate the prophetic methodology of the Old Testament, one from the Psalter and one from the prophet Hosea.

Psalm 22 is not a prediction, but a lament. There we read of the psalmist's suffering and how he would be abandoned by all, surrounded by his foes and deprived of everything, including his very clothes. But the lament applies so minutely to the life of Christ that it is impossible to judge the coinciding details as simply a

---

apocalyptic literature, invented the character as did the author of the Book of Judith.

62 In this way the Daniel of the Book of Daniel would resemble Job: we know little about the historical Job, for the Book of Job supplies him with no genealogy. An additional note at the end of the book in the Septuagint version identifies Job with Jobab (Job 42:16 LXX), suggesting that the Edomite Jobab (found in Gen. 36:33) formed the historical basis for the poetic character found in the Book of Job.

63 The ways in which the Old Testament foretells Christ I examined in *The Christian Old Testament: Looking at the Hebrew Scriptures through Christian Eyes* (Chesterton, IN: Ancient Faith Publishing, 2012).

coincidence. Thus the psalm opens with the very cry of Jesus from the Cross, and the taunts of the psalmist's foes are the very words echoed by those who stood around Jesus and watched Him die (Ps. 22:8; Matt. 27:43). Jesus was also literally surrounded by His foes and was literally despoiled of His very clothes by those who cast lots for them (Ps. 22:18; Matt. 27:35). The psalmist may not have been predicting, yet when the life of Christ is laid over this psalm like a grid, it fits exactly.

Or take the words of Hosea 11:1, where we read of God's protection and love for Israel. "When Israel was a child, I loved him, and out of Egypt I called my son." Again we see not prediction, but poetry, for Hosea here was not predicting the coming Messiah or giving future details from the life of Christ. Rather, he was describing God's care of His people and how He loved them as a father loves his son, bringing them out of Egypt at the exodus. Yet when one lays the details of Christ's life over this prophecy, one again sees an exact fit, for Jesus was God's Son whom He quite literally brought out of Egypt (Matt. 2:14–15).

In the same way as these prophecies reveal Christ to discerning eyes, the Book of Daniel also reveals Him. When one reads that a small stone was cut from a mountain without human hands, and that this stone would ultimately end the world order and fill the world (Dan. 2:34–35), it is impossible not to think of Christ. He was born supernaturally of the Virgin Mary, even as the stone was taken supernaturally from the mountain. He will end the world order when He comes in glory at His Second Coming. It is His Kingdom that will one day fill the world, a Kingdom which will never be destroyed (Dan. 2:44). The Fathers consistently interpreted this as being fulfilled in Jesus, and they were not wrong.

Another patristic commonplace is the identification of the fourth figure in Nebuchadnezzar's fiery furnace with the preincarnate

Christ. Such an identification was natural, given that the king declares that "the appearance of the fourth is like *uio theo*," rendered in the Protestant Authorized Version, the Roman Catholic Douay Version, and the Orthodox Study Bible as "the Son of God." St. Jerome was among the Fathers who questioned the identification, and we have seen that the Aramaic will not allow such a translation. The Greek reproduced above is from the Theodotion version, rendered by one modern translation[64] as "a divine son" (the Old Greek of the original Septuagint reads "a divine angel"). Nevertheless, as Jerome allowed, it was too close to the Christological title and too good a typology not to at least foreshadow Christ the Son of God, and the Church in her hymns has quite properly made the most of it. When the disciples of Christ fall into the fiery furnaces of their own times, be they furnaces of persecution or temptation, He does not abandon them, but stays with them to preserve them unharmed and transform the fire into refreshing dew.

We see the same fulfillment in Christ in the vision of the son of man. In the original vision, the term "son of man" simply meant "a human being," for the coming kingdom of the saints of the Most High (Dan. 7:22, 27) was to be as different from the previous pagan kingdoms as men are different from beasts. The figure of the son of man in the vision coalesces with that of the people of God. And this is exactly and prophetically right, for Jesus, who used the title "the Son of Man" as His favorite self-designation, also identifies with His people, for the Church is His Body, and to persecute the Church is to persecute Him (compare Acts 9:4–5).

The image here in Daniel of the human being, the son of man, was soon enough taken over by the Book of Enoch to identify not a people, but an individual, the Messiah himself, and it is from this

---

64   *A New English Translation of the Septuagint*, edited by Albert Pietersma and Benjamin G. Wright (Oxford: Oxford University Press, 2007).

trajectory that Jesus took the title as His favorite one. When the son of man in Dan. 7:13f is brought before the ancient of days on the clouds of heaven, this finds graphic and literal fulfillment in the glorified Christ coming before the Father to receive the Kingdom, and it is not surprising therefore that Christ interpreted these verses in precisely this way at His trial (Matt. 26:64). Thereafter to Jesus "was given dominion and glory and kingdom, that all peoples, nations, and languages should serve Him." He is the true Son of Man, and we saints only receive the Kingdom because we are in Him.

Finally, we note the Christological dimensions of the vision of the seventy weeks. As noted above, both the timing of the vision (beginning with Jeremiah's word/the beginning of the exile) and the horror with which the cessation of the offering is greeted throughout the Book of Daniel make it impossible that Jesus Christ is the main referent in the original vision. But Christ provides the final fulfillment of the vision nonetheless. The angel promised that after the desolator of the temple had been destroyed, everlasting righteousness would be ushered in. In the terms of the Book of Daniel, this was to come after Antiochus Epiphanes was removed.

In fact, the world still awaits the coming of everlasting righteousness, for it will only come with Christ when He returns in glory. As far as timing is concerned, therefore, the vision focused upon Antiochus, but the hope it held out finds its fulfillment in Christ. The vision of the seventy weeks is thus like all the other visions in that the hoped-for end of this age and the coming of God's glory are fulfilled in the Lord Jesus and His coming Kingdom. Once again the traditional patristic understanding of this passage proves correct. The deepest significance of the Book of Daniel, like everything else in the Old Testament, is profoundly Christological.

The Perennial Message of the Book of Daniel

One might perhaps imagine that because the Book of Daniel was a tract for its own times, it now has nothing to say to ours. Nothing could be further from the truth, for the message of the Book of Daniel becomes more relevant and urgent with every passing day.

As mentioned above, the days of the second century BC were dark ones for God's people, as King Antiochus's reign of terror threatened to annihilate faithfulness from the land and wipe out remembrance of God from the people. Such a reign precipitated a crisis of faith for the pious, and the Book of Daniel was offered to them by the wise as the answer. Drawing possibly from older sources and tales (some scholars have discerned an older Persian atmosphere in the adventure stories), a soul on fire with apocalyptic vision in the second century BC combined these stories of courage and perseverance during the exile with visions of coming deliverance. The resultant book, with both adventure stories and visions, had a single urgent message: Let the faithful hold fast. As God once delivered Daniel and his friends, so He will deliver us now. The pagan kings of the world have always been fools, buffoons unable to see that the Most High rules over the nations. Do not fear Antiochus. Fear God. Soon Antiochus will be broken by no human hand, and God's eternal Kingdom will be established in the earth.

It is true that Antiochus Epiphanes has come and gone, and we still await that promised Kingdom. But it is important that we read the visions as intended—not as predictions, but parables; not offering a timetable, but assurance. The courageous apocalyptic writers who produced and preached the Book of Daniel were not wrong in their message that their God could be trusted. The visions of Daniel were not given to send us scrambling for calendars and calculators to discover in advance when the end will be and when the Lord will restore the kingdom to Israel (Acts 1:6–7). Many have done so in the past, sometimes even predicting a date for the Second Coming, thereby adding an embarrassing comedic element to the history of biblical interpretation.

Such things are fixed by God's own authority, and He does not divulge to us times or seasons, even in prophecies. All of the Book of Daniel is prophetic, and it is the characteristic of prophecy not to reveal fine details of the future, but to call men to repentance and faithfulness in the present. We misunderstand prophecy if we imagine it to contain minute and detailed predictions, for that was never God's way. The prophecies of the Hebrew prophets were not history written in advance, but the cry of the watchman, warning from the walls. The details of the future were not fixed but allowed for men's repentance (compare Jonah 3:4–10).

In this book, God tells us that the evil of tyrants will one day pass away, and that the kingdom of the world will become the Kingdom of our Lord and of His Christ (Rev. 11:15). It is a perennial message and one relevant to every epoch and generation, for every generation produces its own tyranny. Nebuchadnezzar, Belshazzar, and Antiochus never die. The book must be applied afresh in every generation.

We see that this is in fact how the book has been used. The Jews smarting under the tyranny of Rome's lash in the first century AD applied the Book of Daniel to their own age, identifying the fourth beast with Rome. (Such was the approach of Josephus and the author of 2 Esdras, even though the latter acknowledged that this interpretation was comparatively new.) Many of the Fathers too identified the fourth beast with Rome and the little horn with the final Antichrist, whom they expected to emerge from the Roman Empire before its disappearance.

The Lord Jesus Himself, in teaching about the horrific desecration of the temple in AD 70, which came as divine judgment for Jerusalem's rejection of Him, invoked the image of the abomination of desolation "as spoken by the prophet Daniel" (Matt. 24:15). Note: the First Book of Maccabees identified the abomination of desolation with that erected by Antiochus (1 Macc. 1:54), yet here the Lord applied the outrage to His own day. There is no need to choose between the two interpretations. Antiochus supplied the primary reference but not the final one. Everything in the life of Christ found echoing foreshadows in the Old Testament Scriptures, including the desolation prophesied by Daniel. When Jerusalem rejected Him, this disastrous abomination would find its fulfillment in their own time.[65]

Listening to the newscasts, opening the newspapers, and surveying the global scene leads one to conclude that a great darkness is descending. No one can predict the future, but one needs only open eyes to see that these are perilous times for Christians. A mighty tide is flowing against us, and it is as if Antiochus Epiphanes stirs in his long sleep. Nebuchadnezzar is very much alive, loudly demanding from the disciples of Jesus that they conform to modern cultural norms and worship the freakish image he has set up. The fiery furnace has been lit and burns hotly, waiting for those who will not conform.

But we have read the Book of Daniel and are among the wise who understand (Dan. 12:10). We will reply to the king that we have no need to cower before him. If He wills, our God whom we serve is able to deliver us from the burning fiery furnace. But if He does not, let all men everywhere know that we will not serve other gods or worship the golden image. Let the world do its worst. The Son of God will be with us in the fire. With Him by our side, we will be safe, and walk free, and sing.

---

65 A parallel example would be the blindness of the Pharisees: Isaiah's denunciation of Israel's blindness in his own day (Is. 6:9f) would also find prophetic fulfillment in the blindness of the Pharisees when they rejected Jesus (Matt. 13:13f).

Works Consulted

Baldwin, Joyce, *Daniel: an Introduction and Commentary*, in Tyndale Old Testament Commentaries (Downer's Grove, Illinois: InterVarsity Press, 1978).

Collins, John, *Daniel: a Commentary on the Book of Daniel* (Minneapolis: Fortress Press, 1993).

Goldingay, John E., *Daniel*, in Word Biblical Commentary (Dallas: Word Books, 1989).

Hartman, Louis, and Alexander DiLella, The Book of Daniel, in *The Anchor Bible* (Garden City, NY: Doubleday & Company, 1978).

Leupold, H. C., *Exposition of Daniel* (Grand Rapids, MI: Baker Book House, 1949).

Lucas, Ernest, *Daniel*, in Apollos Old Testament Commentary (Downer's Grove, Illinois: InterVarsity Press, 2002).

McDowell, Josh, *Prophecy Fact or Fiction, Historical Evidence for the Authenticity of the Book of Daniel* (San Bernardino, CA: Campus Crusade for Christ, 1979).

Pace, Sharon, *Daniel*, in Smyth & Helwys Bible Commentary (Macon, GA: Smyth & Helwys Publishing Co., 2008).

Porteous, Norman, *Daniel, a Commentary*, in The Old Testament Library (Philadelphia: The Westminster Press, 1965).

Rowley, H. H., *Darius the Mede and the Four World Empires in the Book of Daniel: A Historical Study of Contemporary Theories* (Cardiff: University of Wales Press, 1964).

Wilson, Robert Dick, *Studies in the Book of Daniel*, Vol. 1 (Grand Rapids, MI: Baker Book House, original 1917, reprinted 1972).

Whitcomb, John C., *Darius the Mede, a Study in Historical Identification* (Philadelphia: The Presbyterian and Reformed Publishing Company, 1963).

Wiseman, D. J. with T. C. Mitchell, R. Joyce, W. J. Martin, and K. A. Kitchen, *Notes of some problems in the Book of Daniel* (London: The Tyndale Press, 1965).

Young, E. J, *The Prophecy of Daniel, A Commentary* (Grand Rapids, MI.: Wm. B. Eerdmans Publishing Co., 1949).

The following journal articles were also consulted:

Walton, John, "The Four Kingdoms of Daniel," in the *Journal of Evangelical Theology* 29/1 (March 1986).

Walton, John, "The Decree of Darius the Mede in Daniel 6," in the *Journal of Evangelical Theology* 31/3 (September 1988).

More Books by Lawrence R. Farley
from Ancient Faith Publishing

The Orthodox Bible Study Companion Series

The Gospel of Matthew: Torah for the Church
• Paperback, 392 pages (ISBN 978-0-9822770-7-2)

The Gospel of Mark: The Suffering Servant
• Paperback, 280 pages (ISBN 978-1-888212-54-9)

The Gospel of Luke: Good News for the Poor
• Paperback, 432 pages (ISBN 978-1-936270-12-5)

The Gospel of John: Beholding the Glory
• Paperback, 376 pages (ISBN 978-1-888212-55-6)

The Acts of the Apostles: Spreading the Word
• Paperback, 352 pages (ISBN 978-1-936270-62-0)

The Epistle to the Romans: A Gospel for All
• Paperback, 208 pages (ISBN 978-1-888212-51-8)

First and Second Corinthians: Straight from the Heart
• Paperback, 319 pages (ISBN 978-1-888212-53-2)

Words of Fire: The Early Epistles of St. Paul to the Thessalonians and the Galatians
• Paperback, 172 pages (ISBN 978-1-936270-02-6)

The Prison Epistles: Philippians, Ephesians, Colossians, Philemon
• Paperback, 224 pages (ISBN 978-1-888212-52-5)

Shepherding the Flock: The Pastoral Epistles of St. Paul the Apostle
to Timothy and Titus
• Paperback, 144 pages (ISBN 978-1-888212-56-3)

The Epistle to the Hebrews: High Priest in Heaven
• Paperback, 184 pages (ISBN 978-1-936270-74-3)

Universal Truth: The Catholic Epistles of James, Peter,
Jude, and John
• Paperback, 232 pages (ISBN 978-1-888212-60-0)

The Apocalypse of St. John: A Revelation of Love and Power
• Paperback, 240 pages (ISBN 978-1-936270-40-8)

Other Books

Let Us Attend: A Journey through the Orthodox Divine Liturgy
• Paperback, 100 pages (ISBN 978-1-888212-87-7)

The Christian Old Testament: Looking at the Hebrew Scriptures
through Christian Eyes
• Paperback, 160 pages (ISBN 978-1-936270-53-8)

The Empty Throne: Reflections on the History and Future
of the Orthodox Episcopacy
• Paperback, 152 pages (ISBN 978-1-936270-61-3)

Following Egeria: A Visit to the Holy Land through Time and Space
• Paperback, 160 pages (ISBN 978-1-936270-21-7)

One Flesh: Salvation through Marriage in the Orthodox Church
• Paperback, 160 pages (ISBN 978-1-936270-66-8)

Unquenchable Fire: The Traditional Christian Teaching about Hell
• Paperback, 240 pages (ISBN 978-1-944967-18-5)

Ancient Faith Publishing hopes you have enjoyed and benefited from this book. The proceeds from the sales of our books only partially cover the costs of operating our nonprofit ministry—which includes both the work of **Ancient Faith Publishing** and the work of **Ancient Faith Radio**. Your financial support makes it possible to continue this ministry both in print and online. Donations are tax-deductible and can be made at **www. ancientfaith.com.**

To request a catalog of other publications,
please call us at (800) 967-7377 or (219) 728-2216
or log onto our website: **store.ancientfaith.com**

 **ANCIENT FAITH RADIO**

Bringing you Orthodox Christian music, readings,
prayers, teaching, and podcasts 24 hours a day since 2004
at
www.ancientfaith.com